MAP YOUR
FINANCIAL
FREEDOM

CHARTING A COURSE
THROUGH ADULTHOOD AND RETIREMENT

PATRICK A. LYONS

ACKNOWLEDGMENTS

First, and foremost, I want to thank you, the reader, for your support. I am honored that you have chosen to buy my book and hope that after reading, you will add it to your personal library and will refer to it often as you tackle the financial challenges of life.

Kelly Starling Lyons, my wife, thank you for being a sounding board for my ideas for this book and the last one. Your insight helped me keep "the jargon" out and write in an easy-to understand format. I could not have done it without you. I love you.

To my daughter, Jordan Lyons, thank you for loving me and making me take breaks from writing to go outside and play to appreciate the precious jewel that you are. You will always be "Daddy's little girl."

To my son, Joshua Lyons, thank you for allowing me to see the lighter side of life. When I watch you never willing to take "No" for an answer, I see a bit of myself in you.

To my parents, Gwendolyn Arline Lyons and Charlie Lyons, two of my biggest supporters, I will never be able to repay you for all you have given me. Thank you for all of your love and for keeping me grounded. You are both genuine inspirations for writing this book.

To my big brother, Charlie James Lyons, Jr., thanks for being the best brother and best friend anyone could ask for. You are one of the smartest people I know, and I don't think I could ever explain in words how much you mean to me.

To my grandmother, "Mur," still going strong after over 90 years, you are one of the finest women I know. You are a woman of great character, and you've always inspired me.

I'd also like to acknowledge the hard work of people behind the scenes. This book would not have come together without them, and I am grateful for their contributions. Thanks to my editor, Catherine Van Herrin, for bringing my words together. Thanks to Tracy Carr, who did an outstanding job with the layout. Thanks to Amie Brooks for the eye-catching cover. I enjoyed working with each of you on Map Your Financial Future and appreciate your hard work on Map Your Financial Freedom as well.

There are many others who mean so much to me and have supported me in countless ways. Although you are not mentioned by name, know that you are remembered in my heart.

TABLE OF CONTENTS

TABLE OF CONTENTS

To my son Joshua,
my Mom Gwendolyn A. Lyons,
and Grandmother Ida Arline.
Thanks for your love, support
and inspiration.

INTRODUCTION

How many times in the last year or more have you heard or been reminded that managing your financial life is much harder today than it was for our parents, or just five years ago? Some of us are fortunate enough to have friends and family to help guide us in important money matters, but for those who don't have such an opportunity, *Map Your Financial Freedom* will serve as the guide and the one handbook that will help you simplify the complicated financial issues in your life today.

You can be a business major in college, but you will likely never take a personal financial management class. Most schools simply do not offer them. And parents either don't always feel comfortable sharing financial matters with their children, or they expect them to learn the ropes at school.

So here you are, all grown up, and you don't have a clue as to how to stretch your limited funds to pay for the ever-increasing bills that show up in your mailbox every day. To make matters worse, it is so easy to pick up bad habits, like using a credit card for frivolous purchases. Before long, those little purchases that weren't paid off end up being a mountain of debt that is tough – if not impossible, in some cases -- to overcome. And, again, if you've been keeping up with the news for the past two years or so, banks, credit unions and credit card companies don't help by adding fees or increasing the interest rates on your accounts with no advance notice, which can really set you back even further in your quest to pay down debts.

Then of course there are those dubious yet enticing emails, pop-ups, or mail offers promising huge commissions to help someone move cash from one country to another, or the ones promising you a college degree of your choice without any class work or exams. You just need to pay a small fee and provide some basic identification so the scammer can steal your identity.

Three years ago, when I published *Map your Financial Future: Starting the Right Path in Your Teens and Twenties*, I discussed the importance of getting on the right path financially at a young age. But it doesn't matter whether you are in your 30s, 40s or 60s – in today's economy, you can always make financial missteps. In fact, I often hear people of all ages say, "I don't have enough money to start investing," or "I am buried in debt and I don't know what to do," among many other excuses to not improve their financial situations.

Because our economic climate has changed so dramatically since I wrote *Map Your Financial Future* three years ago, I realized the need for another perspective on this subject. I sincerely thank all the readers who gave me such positive feedback on *Map Your Financial Future;* I took those comments and incorporated additional, updated, real-world examples, tables, and charts to bring home the specific ways in which you can use certain techniques and tools to navigate through your own financial journey.

As you'll read later in this book, there are many ways to start saving -- even in small increments. The important thing is to take control of your financial future today. Don't keep telling yourself you'll do it, but not until tomorrow, next week, or the first of the next month. Financial procrastination leads to self-pity, which then leads to failure.

You can have the financial freedom you deserve, and this book will help you attain that.

A NOTE ON PRIDE

Pride gets a bad rap sometimes. But it can be a pathway to success. I have turned the word PRIDE into an acronym for a formula to win in life:

"P" stands for **preparation**. Good fortune is hardly ever the result of luck. To be successful in any endeavor requires hard work and training.

"R" stands for **respect**. Honor yourself and elders. I went through a phase where I felt I knew everything. Our parents, grandparents, and others have knowledge that should be used to our advantage. They have gone through many of life's challenges that we have yet to face.

"I" stands for **individualism**. Leaders never follow the crowd. They stand out because they have vision and are willing to take risks.

"D" stands for **discipline**. Once you have a plan, stick with it and stay the course no matter how tough things become. In life, things rarely go as planned. We can succeed by being patient, believing in ourselves, and moving forward with our goals.

If you can live by the principles of **Preparation, Respect, Individualism,** and **Discipline,** you will **Excel** in life, which is what the **"E"** stands for.

HOW DO YOU USE THIS BOOK?

Map Your Financial Freedom is divided into four main sections. The first part is focused on the basics of budgeting. Part two discusses credit and how to navigate this resource while avoiding the landmines. Part three stresses the importance of continuing your education even after getting settled into your career, as well as steps to help you start your own business if you have the entrepreneurial bug. Part four covers the myriad ways of building a nest egg as well as estate planning. Each chapter ends with a summary, "Things to Remember," to cover the most important topics.

Planning your financial future can be challenging, but having a "map" to guide you can and will make the journey so much easier. This book will offer you the tools to plot your path with financial savvy so that you will have a clear plan to help achieve all of your financial goals.

PART 1

CHAPTER 1

BUDGETING

Budgeting is among the number-one things most people do not want to hear about, talk about, or think about, but the following message is tried-and-true.

Developing a budget is the first step to achieving financial freedom. It's as simple as that! The thing is, most of us think a "budget" has to be complicated or prepared by someone skilled in managing money, but it's just not true – it's simply taking stock of your everyday expenses; your long-term expenses and investments, your monthly or quarterly payment plans, and your "hidden expenses" – those often not-so-little fees that crop up when you least expect it, like the need for a new set of tires, an emergency plane trip, or a sudden leaky roof or other home maintenance need. A budget is simply a plan that helps guide you in reaching your financial goals. It's like a blueprint is to a builder. Without it, he can not construct a building. Without a budget, you can't plan for retirement.

Also, though self-discipline is required to follow a budget, it has some wiggle room, too. You just have to balance your "wants" and "needs" a lot more closely in order to maximize your income.

If you find that your initial plan is too restrictive, then by all means, adjust it. Having a budget means making choices. After all, you are the one in charge of your finances. For example, maybe you can choose to attend just one party instead of going out every night of the week. And certainly you can still treat yourself to a pair of new shoes, but just look for a sale instead of paying full price.

SETTING UP A BUDGET

A budget can be very basic: It essentially provides an estimate of the money coming in and the money paid out in your expenses. It is designed to show you where your money is going and keep you from spending more than you bring home. Simple enough so far, right?

As an example, I set my first budget by making a list of all of my expenses and tracking them with a computer spreadsheet program. After monitoring these expenses for a couple of months, I became more aware of exactly how much my bills were and was thus able to make good estimates of what they would be in the future. With that information, I gave myself an allowance. This was spending money I could use for things I wanted to buy after my bills were paid. But once I spent my allowance, that was it. I set up a system for myself in which I had to wait until my next paycheck arrived before allowing myself more pocket money. And that was a good experience, because during this process, I actually learned how to stretch my allowance!

Because I realized it's important to reward yourself for meeting your financial goals, as I paid off a debt or got a raise, I gave myself a slight raise in my allowance. Then, I used that money to buy whatever I wanted or needed most. Please, if you take one thing away from this book, remember this and imprint it in your mind: A budget is not a bad word; it is not a punishment. You may not believe me now, but you can actually turn this into a sort of self-competitive game – you can make room for fun while you're planning for the future.

The worksheet below will help you construct a budget. List all of your expenses. If you go to Starbucks to get a latte in the morning or go by McDonald's to get a combo meal for lunch, record those costs on the form. Save receipts if you have to; don't let the hustle and bustle of the world let you lose track of any expense, no matter how small. If you commit to it, this exercise will really work like a financial "diet" – it will help you find areas to "trim."

Rent and/or mortgage payments tend to be the largest expense category for most people. If after cutting back on smaller expenses, you find you don't have enough income to pay your bills, consider finding a smaller place to live or getting a roommate to share the bills. As a rule of thumb, mortgage/rent payment should not exceed 32% of your gross income. So if you are making $2,000 a month before taxes, your rent or mortgage payment should be no more than $640 per month.

I found that keeping a record of my bills and purchases in a structured format, like the one below, made me think twice before charging something I could not afford:

Sample Expense Worksheet

Date	Store	Item	Cost
3-Aug	American Eagle	Jeans	$198
4-Aug	McDonalds	Chicken Combo	$5
7-Aug	BP	Gas	$25
15-Aug	Foot Locker	Shoes	$80
17-Aug	Starbucks	Hot Cocoa	$3
19-Aug	Applebee's	Hamburger	$8
19-Aug	Ben & Jerry's	Ice Cream	$4
21-Aug	Jaluka Juice	Smoothie	$5
23-Aug	Ticketmaster	2 concert tickets	$60
23-Aug	Honda	Oil change	$30
24-Aug	The Moon	Party	$20
		Monthly Total	$448

Sample Monthly Budget

	Budget Amount	Actual Amount	Budget -Actual
INCOME			
Paycheck	$2,000.00	$2,000.00	$0.00
Business Income	$0.00	$0.00	$0.00
Total Income	$2,000.00	$2,000.00	$0.00
EXPENSES			
Car payment	$250.00	$250.00	$0.00
Rent	$560.00	$560.00	$0.00
Car Insurance	$70.00	$70.00	$0.00
Groceries	$100.00	$120.00	($20.00)
Cell Phone	$50.00	$75.00	($25.00)
Utilities	$120.00	$130.00	($10.00)
Entertainment	$200.00	$300.00	($100.00)
Credit card	$100.00	$120.00	($20.00)
Donations - Church	$200.00	$200.00	$0.00
Savings	$100.00	$175.00	($75.00)
Total Expenses	$1,750.00	$2,000.00	($250.00)
Income minus expenses	$250.00	$0.00	$0.00

PERSONAL FINANCE SOFTWARE PROGRAMS

In 1997, I started using Microsoft Money computer software to keep track of my finances. If you are computer-savvy, I highly recommend using a personal finance package such as Money or Quicken. These programs can help you set a budget, establish a retirement savings plan, set up a debt reduction strategy, and balance your checkbook.

Microsoft Money takes the financial information you enter and generates reports showing where your money is going. One time, the program made a note that my dining-out expenses jumped from 5% of my monthly expenses to 12%. This little "red flag" prompted me to get cooking lessons from my mom so I could learn to make foods that I like and use the leftovers for my lunch. I also tried to find more reasonably priced restaurants when I ate out for lunch and dinner.

After about six months of using Money, I realized that I had exceeded my budget several times. It was time for some serious thought – I had to determine whether my budget or my spending habits needed adjustments. Here's a clue to determine which one needs tweaking: If your income is the same but your expenses are growing, then you need to reduce your spending. If you have some leeway after your bills are paid and find that your current plan is too rigid, it's OK to increase your budget.

Another reason to modify your budget is if some of your monthly recurring bills, like car insurance, rent and utilities, have increased. If you don't want to change your plan, shop around for better deals. Every dollar spent on essential bills is one dollar less for the things you want to do. Here's a simple rule of thumb to remember: When your income equals expenses, it is called a balanced budget.

The ease of acquiring credit cards these days has allowed many people to spend more and more – even when they don't have enough income and savings to afford to buy the things they do. So when expenses exceed income, we are in a deficit. Stated another way, we are living beyond our means. If the problem is allowed to worsen, it can turn into a disaster and lead to bankruptcy.

According to the American Bankruptcy Institute, more than 1 million people filed for bankruptcy in 2008. Bankruptcy occurs when you have more expenses than income and have no other choice but to petition the Federal Court system for either reorganization or liquidation. Bankruptcy should always be a last resort. The term "reorganization" means the government will come up with a plan to lower payments on your debts so you can still pay them off. "Liquidation" means your obligation to pay your debts is essentially wiped away. In either case, the consequences are not good, because a bankruptcy filing remains on your credit report for ten years. (See Chapters four and five for more information on credit reports and bankruptcy.)

EMERGENCY FUND

Remember that leaky roof? A blown-out tire that needs to be replaced? Unexpected expenses are a fact of life. Let's say you get laid off. With the loss of your job comes the loss of your health insurance. What do you do if you have a medical emergency or need prescription medications while you are laid off? Then, there are those unexpected car and home repairs. In these and other circumstances, credit cards and other loans can be a source of taking care of bills. But there's another and much wiser option: Establish an emergency fund before the problems occur!

Setting up an emergency fund can really help you reduce the need to use credit when you're in a bind. Instead of reaching for your charge card, you can just withdraw money from the account you've reserved for these special circumstances. It's a good idea to work toward building a balance equal to four to six months of living expenses. The funds should be invested in a money market or savings account because these pay more interest than a typical checking account. Money market accounts are also good because in cases of emergencies, you can get to the funds relatively quickly.

Saving four to six months of expenses may sound like a difficult goal. But you can get started by depositing a portion of each paycheck in this account. Start small and increase contributions as you're able. It will take some time to build your emergency fund, but this is always a step in the right direction.

SPLURGE FUND

Certainly everyone enjoys (and likely deserves) a spending spree once in a while, and don't think that just because you are on a budget, you can't ever have those "special treats" any more. One way to keep your budget under control is by setting up a splurge fund. Money in this account can be used on whatever you want. I suggest setting up a money market account or a savings account (both typically pay more interest than a checking account), and then take a close look at your budget to determine how much you can afford to put in your annual splurge fund.

For instance, if you would like to reward yourself with $1,200 each year for special purchases or impulse buys, make monthly deposits of $100. Next, choose how often you would like to go on these shopping sprees and come up with a withdrawal schedule. Using the Sample Monthly Budget above, under "Entertainment" and "Savings," you can withdraw $300 every three months to send yourself on a quarterly shopping spree ($1,200/4 = $300).

MONEY-SAVING TIPS

You may be saying, "Well, sure, that sounds all fine and good, but I don't have the kind of job that pays enough for me to save any money."

Here's where I must make a correction: You can save money! Yes, you can! Although you may not yet be making the income you wish, there are plenty of ways to stretch your dollars without sacrificing the quality of your life. The categories below include several examples, and they're easier than you think – I guarantee it.

CLOTHING

Most Americans spend a lot on clothes. OK, let's face it: Most Americans probably spend too much on clothes! But one way to save on clothes is to really check out the clearance racks. These clothes are usually in good shape but simply may be out of season, so retailers lower the prices to move them out the door more quickly to make room for their seasonal merchandise. You may have to spend more time searching, but you'll walk out the store happier for spending much less than you would had you bought "in season" clothing.

Outlet malls are another great source for bargains. They offer many name-brand items, but at lower prices than you can find at shopping malls, which basically send all their "overstock" merchandise to outlets. The clothes might have slight imperfections that the mall stores could not sell at full price, either, but so many of these are so minor, they're either barely noticeable or they're easy to cover up with accessories such as jewelry, scarves, or even your hair! Your own imagination can save you lots of cash!

One other very good place to shop for clothes on a budget is at consignment, or "second-hand" stores or boutiques. These are usually smaller, independent-run stores that will most definitely have "originals" that someone else is going to be wearing – and that's because the clothes in consignment stores are those that other people have found no more use for but are quite often still in excellent shape. So, when you buy your Manolo Blahniks or Barker Blacks at $35 a pair, the woman or man who barely wore them before you gets a "take" or a partial payment from that sale.

This strategy also can work in reverse: Scour your own closet for clothes you don't wear any more because you've either outgrown them, you simply have never liked them, or they were given to you from a well-meaning friend who didn't quite get your size right. Take those to the consignment shop after making sure they are clean and pressed, and put them on consignment. This way, you'll be profiting from unused or unwearable clothes of your own.

TRANSPORTATION

Despite all the talk about moving to renewable energy sources, gas prices continue to climb in this economy. One way to shave transportation costs is to use regular unleaded gasoline instead of premium. Unless your vehicle specifically calls for premium gas, you can save 20 cents a gallon or more by simply using a lower grade of fuel. If your vehicle has a 14-gallon tank, the savings could be about $3 a week, which adds up to approximately $150 per year. This savings could be applied to other expenses. Also, having your tires properly inflated provides less road resistance and can help improve gas mileage. Taking it easy on the gas pedal can also save on fuel costs.

Another area to consider is the size of your vehicle. Some vendors charge more for scheduled maintenance on larger vehicles. Also, though very popular just five years ago, today many people are trading in their gas-guzzling sport utility vehicles for smaller, more fuel-efficient cars. As a general rule of thumb, the longer and/or larger the vehicle, the worse the gas mileage. Let's use Ford vehicles as an example. A Ford Expedition, which is a large sport utility automobile, gets 14 miles per gallon in the city. The Ford Escape, a compact size sport utility, gets 18 to 22 miles per gallon in the city. The Ford Focus, a compact car, gets 26 miles per gallon in the city. Switching from an Expedition to the Focus could cut your fuel costs by almost 50%.

Hybrid vehicles are another way to save on fuel costs. Hybrids use a combination of fuel and electricity to provide better gas mileage than conventional cars. Some hybrids, such as the Toyota Prius, are reputed to deliver 60 miles per gallon in the city. Currently, hybrids cost more than comparable conventional vehicles, but prices are expected to drop as car manufacturers continue to become more efficient at the manufacturing process.

WHOLESALE CLUBS

Wholesale clubs such as BJ's, Costco, and Sam's Club can be a great source for finding a wide variety of bargains on household items. These membership clubs usually require an annual fee to join, but if you're a dedicated shopper at one of these clubs, you can recoup those costs fairly quickly. Some may also require that you work for a certain company or be a member of a particular organization. These clubs can offer prices lower than typical grocery and retail stores because they buy in bulk and are able to get favorable rates. Then, they pass some of the savings on to their members.

Some of these clubs may require you to buy in large quantities to get the savings, but stores like Costco give its members the option to buy in smaller amounts. If you are planning a party or cookout and need to buy in bulk, wholesale clubs can provide considerable savings over grocery store prices. Also, some of these organizations offer discounts on products and services such as gas, car maintenance, eyeglasses and travel, as well.

ONLINE SHOPPING

Online shopping is becoming increasingly popular among consumers because companies who list their services on the Internet typically offer lower prices than traditional stores. Expenses for Internet retailers are less than "brick and mortar" stores because there are minimal overhead costs. In other words, not being typical "stores," they don't have to pay to keep the lights and air-conditioning or heat on. Online retailers do use warehouses for their products, but again, they don't have to employ people to staff a traditional store. So, you save money simply because the cost of running an online store is often much less expensive for the owners and require fewer people and man hours than a typical retail store.

You can find great deals online in just about every category. When it comes to travel, websites like Expedia, Priceline and Travelocity offer discounts on airfare, hotel accommodations, and rental cars. Major airlines and hotel chains also offer specials that are only available for online shoppers. In addition, Internet auction sites like eBay can offer tremendous savings compared to retail stores. I have made a habit of searching eBay before I buy certain items like electronic items or books. There is an old saying that "one man's trash is another man's treasure." I have found new and rarely used products on eBay and saved more than 50% compared to retail prices. That's even counting shipping costs!

You can also go to online auction sites to find great gift ideas at a fraction of the retail cost for just about any occasion. While these sites can be a great way of saving money, here you have to be more watchful for the danger of fraud. One way to lessen this risk is to look at a member's feedback rating before bidding on items. On eBay, I tend to only bid on items from members who have a feedback rating of 98% or better and those who have conducted at least 50 transactions. That reassures me that particular member has completed a fair amount of transactions and the majority of the customers were satisfied.

For buying from other online stores, consider using respected retailers like Wal-Mart and Target. Also think about making purchases through websites such as Amazon or Yahoo! before going to the store or mall. These sites have standards that stores must follow to be listed, so this is a pretty safe bet because most retailers do not want to risk being kicked off a large Internet mall. They know it could hurt their sales and damage credibility among their customers.

FINDING A ROOMMATE

If you are just starting out on your own, seeing your bills for the first time can be overwhelming. There's rent or mortgage, utilities (gas, electric, water), and a phone bill. On top of that, there are transportation costs (car payment and gas or public transportation), insurance (auto, life, renters' or homeowners') and, perhaps most important, food! Having a roommate can drastically cut down on the sticker shock of living expenses.

If you choose to get a roommate, be sure to reach a (preferably written) agreement about how the bills will be split and when they will be paid. You truly should consider entering into a written contract. That way, both of you know the rules from the beginning, and if either person defaults on payment, you can prove that you had a written document for civil court purposes, if it has to go that route. A simple, signed sheet of paper can save a lot of frustration down the line.

Sample Budget

	Budget Amount	Actual Amount	Budget Actual
INCOME			
Paycheck/Allowance			
Business Income			
Total Income			
EXPENSES			
Car payment			
Rent			
Car Insurance			
Groceries			
Cell Phone			
Utilities			
Entertainment			
Credit card			
Donations - Church			
Savings			
Total Expenses			
Income minus expenses			

Things to Remember

1. Determine how much money you have coming in. Consider all of your income: paycheck, allowance, other business income, inheritance, monetary gifts, etc.

2. List your expenses, such as rent or mortgage, food, gas, etc. To save yourself a lot of trouble and extra expense, ask yourself this question often: "What do I really need?" and only use your purchasing power for those necessities.

3. Give yourself a reasonable allowance so you can enjoy some of your hard-earned cash; after all, everyone should splurge now and again!

4. Create a money cushion. Ideally, you want to make sure you have some cash left over after paying for essentials to put in a savings account reserved for emergencies.

5. Adjust your spending. If you find that you are spending more than you make, quickly cut your expenses or try to bring in more income.

CHAPTER 2

CHOOSING A FINANCIAL INSTITUTION

Choosing the right financial institution is a very vital, important decision to make.

D
espite the economic fallout, banks and credit unions are still good places to put your money. Opening an account is painless. You simply provide your name, address, date of birth, your social security number, and some other type of identifying document like a driver's license, plus your initial deposit. Then, you're ready to go. But how do you decide whether to stash your cash in a bank account or credit union? Let's go over the benefits and drawbacks of each.

BANKS VERSUS CREDIT UNIONS

By definition, banks are for-profit institutions, meaning they have a vested interest in charging more for products to increase their earnings. Banks can have a national footprint like BankAmerica or be more regional or community-focused.

Credit unions, on the other hand, are non-profit organizations that tend to focus more on a particular region. Credit unions pay dividends (earnings paid out from its profits) to its members. The profits are also used to lower rates that members obtain on loans and increase returns they receive for deposits.

Here's another difference to consider: Banks allow virtually anyone to open an account. Credit unions require a common bond for membership, such as being employed by a certain company or belonging to a particular organization. Additionally, all credit union account-holders share ownership in the credit union and select the board of directors. Having an account at a bank does not make you a shareholder unless you decide to buy stock in that particular company.

One downside of credit unions is the limited availability of Automated Teller Machines (ATMs). Because most credit unions are regionally based, if you travel out of that area, it may be difficult to find an ATM for your credit union. ATM cards are accepted at almost any machine, but most financial institutions charge a fee for customers who use their machines unless you have an account with them.

That's where banks have an edge. If you have an account at a national bank such as Citibank or BankAmerica, there is a greater likelihood you will find an ATM if you are traveling across the country. Many banks and credit unions issue Visa/MasterCard check cards, which allow users to make purchases and have the costs deducted from their checking accounts. In addition, using ATM cards for debit transactions allows consumers to withdraw cash at most retail stores without paying a fee. Just be careful to make sure no one is looking over your shoulder when you enter your personal identification number (PIN), because there is a lot of fraud with ATM/debit cards (See Chapter 6 for more about identity theft.) Whether you choose a bank or credit union, your deposits will be insured up to $250,000, meaning that any balance under that amount is protected even if the financial institution goes out of business.

CHECKING ACCOUNTS

Checking accounts are places to store cash used to pay for expenses. You can access the money two ways: by writing a check or by using an ATM/debit card. There are two basic types of checking accounts: interest-bearing and non-interest bearing. In exchange for paying you interest on your money, interest-bearing accounts require a minimum balance. If your balance falls beneath that level, the financial institution will likely charge a monthly (or even daily) fee until your account returns to your bank's balance requirement. Keep in mind that the interest rate paid on interest-bearing checking accounts is usually not that compelling. It varies depending on market conditions (the national average was 0.64% as of July 22, 2009, according to www.Bankrate.com). Non-interest bearing accounts typically require a low or no minimum balance.

MONEY MARKET ACCOUNTS

A money market account is another type of checking account. These accounts typically pay a higher interest rate than checking or savings accounts (the national average was 1.22% as of July 22, 2009). Money market accounts make investments in short-term funds. The return on the money is passed along to the account holders. This type of account, like interest-bearing checking accounts, usually requires a minimum balance, which can be anywhere from as low as $1 to as high as $50,000.

SAVINGS ACCOUNTS

Savings accounts encourage customers to keep money in their accounts, so they give you an incentive – they offer a higher interest rate than checking accounts. Why would you want to withdraw money from a high-interest-bearing account? This is where you can make money on your own money – where your real savings come into the picture. Withdrawals and deposits are allowed, but no checks can be written against the balance of your savings account in most cases.

BROKERAGE ACCOUNTS

This type of account is set up at an investment bank such as Charles Schwab or TD Ameritrade. Brokerage accounts allow you to buy and sell stocks, bonds, mutual funds, and other investment vehicles. Most brokerage firms also permit customers to write checks against their account balances. (We will discuss brokerage accounts in more detail in Chapter 12.)

ONLINE BANKING

Hate long lines? Feeling overwhelmed by accumulating paper like cancelled checks and monthly statements? Online banking may be for you. It's the option of choice for a growing number of people. You can use features like direct deposit which allow you to have your paycheck deposited directly into your checking account – and this means you'll never need to step into a bank. You can view your bank records online.

Some people worry about online banking because they feel it makes their private information vulnerable to interception. Banks are constantly working to increase online banking security by using encryption software to protect sensitive information from being viewed by others. You can help safeguard your personal information by remembering to click the "exit" or "logoff" button at the end of an online session and close your Internet browser before moving on to another site.

These are some other features you can use through online banking:

- Check account balances.
- View current and historical transactions.
- See the front and back of checks that have been processed.
- Verify withdrawals and deposits.
- Stop payments on checks.
- Study bank statements.
- Transfer funds between accounts.
- Download transactions to popular personal finance programs like Quicken and Microsoft Money.

All of these conveniences cut down on the amount of paper you receive in the mail. If you're like me, one less letter to file or shred helps a lot.

ONLINE BILL PAY

A special feature of online banking that provides convenience and control is online bill pay. This option allows users to receive and pay bills online. Some banks charge for this service, but many are beginning to offer it for free. If you are working full-time and living on your own, online bill pay is worth it even if you have to pay a small monthly fee.

Online bill pay allows you to view your bills and schedule payments. You can always print a bill or bank statement if you want to have a hard copy. In the meantime, you save on postage by not having to buy stamps, and on that pesky clutter, too!

Some online services will even send reminder emails to inform you that a bill is due. This is a great feature. When living on your own for the first time, it's nice to have something to remind you that a bill is due. That nudge can mean the difference between having your lights on or getting them turned off. Restoring a cancelled service means late fees and additional charges to have it turned back on due to late payment.

You can also set up recurring payments for your bills. For ones that are typically the same amount each month like rent or mortgage, cable, or car insurance, setting up a regular payment schedule can save a lot of time. Just specify the day of the month you want the payment to post, and the funds will be sent automatically until or unless you make a change.

VIRTUAL BANKS

Virtual banks are popping up everywhere. These financial institutions have no physical branches or tellers. Everything is handled online. Here again, you will never have to walk into a branch. This option can provide some nice benefits – because these banks don't have to employ tellers and other staff to operate branches, they can pass the savings on to customers in the form of higher interest rates on checking and savings accounts. These entities do hire employees to process checks and other transactions just as any other bank, but there is no physical building. It's the equivalent to an online store, which we covered earlier. Virtual banks also offer ATM cards, but because most don't own ATMs, so there is likely to be a fee every time you make a withdrawal. Another downside to these banks is that deposits can't be made via ATMs, so you may have to resort to using the mail, which can pose some security risks.

One final note on banking: Do your homework and search for the financial institution that will best meet your needs. If you feel comfortable with the Internet and don't need to see a teller, virtual banks could be a good option for you. If you are planning to use a financial institution for loans and credit, credit unions might be the best option since they offer among the lowest rates on credit cards and loans. Their wide array of products and services can also be a selling point. Other factors in your decision could be availability of direct deposit, online banking, and bill pay.

Another consideration is fees. Banks and credit unions may require you to maintain a certain balance or pay a fee if you fall short. I highly recommend finding a firm that does not charge those kinds of penalties. Having to maintain a certain balance can be restrictive and costly. It's also very worrisome, and quite needlessly so, since there are so many other options. Some other fees to consider are wire transfer, stop payment, and overdraft. In my experience and opinion, credit unions are typically cheaper than banks in these fee categories by a wide margin.

Finally, think about convenience. If you will be using ATMs a lot or need to handle transactions in a physical location, choosing a bank with a big presence may be important. Larger banks tend to have more ATMs than smaller banks, which can prevent you from having to pay ATM fees. Credit unions are usually local in nature, so if you do a lot of ATM withdrawals, you may have to do a lot of searching to find one that doesn't charge a fee.

BANK CHARGES

Many banks offer free checking, but don't be fooled: the "free" usually stops right there! Here are some of the fees you may incur if you have a bank account:

- **Insufficient Funds** – One day, you may slip and write a check for more money than you have in your account. When someone tries to cash it, your bank will send you a notice of insufficient funds. That means your check has bounced. Everyone makes mistakes, but be careful not to willfully write bad checks, because along with bank charges -- which can be more than $30 per check -- you could literally go to jail. The best way to keep from racking up bounced checks is to know exactly what's coming in and out of your account on a daily basis.

  If your bank offers online banking, you can login to your account to verify which checks have cleared, thereby giving yourself a safety net. Again, this is yet another great reason to have a savings account, because most banks will use part of that money to serve as overdraft protection.

Another safeguard against bounced checks is considering the time it takes for your bank to make your money available after a deposit. Some banks may not allow you to access your funds for three to five days. If a check comes in during that time frame, it may bounce.

- **Wire Transfer** – Let's say, for example, that you're purchasing a house and need money transferred from your bank account to your lawyer's bank account. For this, you may need to do a wire transfer. Fees for bank wire transfers are as low as $10.

- **Stop Payment** – If you write a check and realize you don't have enough money to cover the amount, you can stop payment on it. Charges often range from $15 to $30 for this service. I realize this sounds high, but by stopping payment you can save the extra, higher fees – and headaches -- from charges for having insufficient funds.

- **ATM Fees** – Think carefully about the ATM you use because you could pay a steep price if you choose one that is not owned by your bank. Some charge convenience fees as much as $5 per session.

- **Minimum Balance Fees** – As I mentioned earlier, some banks charge fees if your checking or savings account balance dips below a certain level. The cost can be high – from $20 or more in some cases.

- **Check Fees** – Some banks allow you to write a certain number of checks each month without a fee. If you exceed that limit, you will be charged a nominal amount such as 25 cents for each check.

Remember to shop around for the best checking account for you. Everyone has individual needs, and banks do work hard to accommodate you – after all, they make money on your interest when you "invest" in their bank! You can find some really good deals out there, and don't hesitate to negotiate an issue – banks really need you; not the other way around. So keep these things in mind when shopping around for the right bank for you – and remember, plenty of banks offering the benefit of free, unlimited check-writing.

OVERDRAFT LOANS

Make sure you read the fine print the next time you sign up for a checking account. Many financial institutions automatically enroll account holders in overdraft programs. These loans are a high-cost form of credit. If you don't have the funds to pay for a purchase you've made by check or your debit card, the bank will pick up the tab, but they'll also charge you a fee for doing so. To illustrate how overdraft programs work, let's look at the table below of debit transactions made over the course of a day. In this scenario, you start the day with $70 in your checking account:

Vendor	Cost	Balance
Beginning Balance	--	$70
Starbucks	$5	$65
Gas	$30	$35
Hamburger Joint (for lunch)	$10	$25
Corner Grocery Store	$30	-$5
Insufficient Funds Charge	$30	-$35
Joe's Bar	$25	-$60
Insufficient Funds Charge	$30	-$90

The transaction at Corner Grocery Store is going to cost you an extra $30 on top of the $30 you spent on groceries. The same holds true for those late-night drinks at Joe's Bar. To put that in perspective, if you are making $10 an hour, it will take you six hours to make up the cost of those two overdrafts. Another thing to consider is that you may have outstanding checks that have not cleared your bank. If you bounce those checks, you will be assessed more fees. You won't receive advance warning from your bank that you are about to overdraw your account. Once you make a deposit into your account, the bank will recover the money it put up for your overdraft plus their fee, which ranges from $20 to $35, according to the Center for Responsible Lending.

Overdraft programs underscore the importance of using a budget to keep track of expenses to avoid overspending. Here are some valuable tips to remember to avoid overdraft charges:

- Check balances daily – Most banks offer online or phone banking so you can check your balance and recent transactions.
- Sign up for an "alert" service with your bank – Banks can send an email to notify you when your balance reaches a certain level. If you receive this notification, it raises a red flag to alert you to cut back on spending until more money is deposited in your account.
- Hold on to receipts – Keep a running total of your expenses during the day so you know what your balance should be, taking into account any outstanding checks you may have.
- Transfer your money from savings or a line of credit – If your checking account balance is low before payday, transfer funds from a savings account or a line of credit until your money is deposited. Then, when you get paid, replenish your savings account or repay your line of credit.
- Designate a savings account for overdraft protection – If you designate a savings account for overdraft purposes, the bank will tap that account if there aren't enough funds in your checking account to cover a transaction. You will still be charged a fee for the overdraft, but it will be much less than the cost for a normal overdraft.

Things to Remember

1. If you decide to use a bank, make sure the deposits are insured by the FDIC. The National Credit Union Administration (NCUA) insures deposits at credit unions. Both of these organizations insure deposits up to $250,000.

2. Find banks with flexible or extended branch hours. Not everyone works from 9 a.m. to 5 p.m. It's nice to have an account at a financial institution that has evening hours or is open during at least the morning hours on weekends.

3. See if the bank offers credit cards. Compare the interest rates with other credit card companies to learn whether the rates are competitive.

4. Ask whether the financial institution offers debit cards that bear either the Visa or MasterCard logo, and find out how the card is protected in the event it is lost or stolen.

5. Investigate the different types of accounts that are offered. You may want to consider a bank that has a wide range of accounts. That way, if your needs change, you have options to meet your requirements without having to change institutions.

6. Determine if the account you open requires a minimum balance. If so, make sure you maintain that amount. If you fall short, you will be charged fees. Some banks waive the minimum balance if you set up a direct deposit of your wages or other income into the account on a monthly basis. Always know where you (and your bank) stand on this issue.

7. Avoid banks that charge fees for withdrawing cash. Why should you pay to get your own money?

PART 2

CHAPTER 3
UNDERSTANDING CREDIT

Getting your first credit card is a pretty heady feeling;
it's almost like a "rite of passage" into adulthood.

Some people get their first taste of credit through offers received at college. Others get advertisements in the mail after landing their first job. Sure, it feels powerful to go into a store and lay down a piece of plastic to pay for purchases. But too few of us consider that the financial choices we make today will directly affect opportunities to buy things that we need in the future.

Now, don't get the wrong idea here: Credit is a good thing if it's managed properly. But so many people, myself included, abuse it at some point in their lives. We make charges without considering the consequences of buying more than we can afford. Out-of-control credit habits can lead to high interest rates and even losing the right to use the card. Think about how much tougher it would to be book an airline ticket, rent a car, or make a hotel reservation without a credit card. And you can almost forget about shopping online.

So make sure you get a strong start by choosing the right card for you. Protect yourself by looking for those with low interest rates. Interest is what credit card companies charge on balances left unpaid after the grace period (the number of days you have to pay your bill in full before accruing extra charges). This grace period typically ranges from one to thirty days.

Next, search for cards with "zero" or low annual fees. An exception to this are reward cards, with which you can earn airline miles, points, or cash back, based on your purchases. If this is important to you, be sure that you will charge enough to make your reward worth more than the fee (which can exceed $100 per year).

It also helps to think of credit cards as loans. The issuer allows you to borrow money to make your purchases, but that company wants something in return. That's where interest comes in. Many companies will drastically increase your interest rate if you pay your bill late. I know of cases in which a 10% interest rate jumped to 30% because of late payment. Paying your credit card bills in full and on time not only boosts your credit score, it's like getting an interest-free loan.

TYPES OF CREDIT

According to www.Wikipedia.com, an online encyclopedia, the financial definition of credit means "the granting of a loan or creation of debt." Loans and other outstanding amounts are of course meant to be repaid. The lender expects to receive the principal amount back, plus interest. For example, if you were to borrow $100 at 10% interest, the bank would expect to get $110 at the end of twelve months. The $100 is the principal amount; the amount that was borrowed. The $10 is the interest, or the bank's charge for letting you borrow the money. A loan is made for a specific time period, and the interest payment is spread equally over the loan. This scenario is an example of simple interest.

Credit cards are a form of revolving credit, which means there are no fixed payments or loan periods. If you have no balance, you owe nothing. But if you have a lot of charges, you could pay for several years before eliminating your debt.

Credit card companies also use compounding interest. That means unless you pay your balance in full, extra interest charges are added each month to what you owe, and that interest is calculated on your new balance. In other words, you are paying interest on interest.

Let's say you have a card with 30% interest, and this interest is compounded daily. This means that for each day it carries a balance, you will be charged 0.08% per day. Sounds like no big deal, right? But as new charges are added, the credit card company will compound more interest on top of that. Before long, you could end up with a huge bill. Consider a $1,000 credit card balance with a 30% interest rate. If you make just a minimum payment of $30 per month, it will take six years to pay off your debt – and that's assuming you make no other charges in the meantime.

One way to keep interest from building is to avoid the trap of the monthly minimum payment. Paying that amount -- just 2% to 4% of your total balance -- can make you feel like you owe less than you really do. This is what credit companies want you to think – it's how they make money off of you, and it's perfectly legal.

Remember, credit cards shouldn't be used to extend your income. If you keep coming up short on money to pay for your charges, stop using that card until you get your finances under control. If you use credit cards for luxuries, such as vacations or holiday gifts, be sure to have a plan to pay off the balance quickly.

When you pay more than the monthly minimum, you are paying down the principal balance of the loan and freeing yourself from the cycle of debt. The lower the principal balance, the less interest the credit card company charges. Here's another way to look at it: The quicker you pay off your balance, the more you save, the more you win. The rule of the game is, you want to stay ahead of the credit card company.

When you receive a credit card in the mail, you'll also receive a document that spells out those legal terms, as well. That's the disclosure statement. Hold on to it. It goes over the benefits and penalties of your credit card. I once heard someone say "the big print giveth and the small print taketh away." Remember to read the fine print. That's where you'll find information about how much your interest rate may increase if you pay your bill late. The tables below highlight the difference an interest rate can make on a $1,000 balance.

For example, credit card A has a 15% interest rate and a monthly minimum payment of $25. If you accrue no additional charges and pay the minimum of $25 a month, you will pay off the $1,000 owed in 56 months (more than four-and-a-half years). The balance will be gone, but consider the cost: you'll have paid an extra $395 in interest! Conversely, if you double your payment to $50 per month, you will pay it off in about two years and pay only $158 in interest.

Credit card A charges 15% interest and has monthly minimum payment of $25

Day	Balance	Payment	Daily Interest	Cumulative Interest
1	$1,000.00			
2	$1,000.41		$0.4110	$0.41
3	$1,000.82		$0.4111	$0.82
4	$1,001.23		$0.4113	$1.23
5	$1,001.64		$0.4115	$1.64
6	$1,002.06		$0.4116	$2.06
7	$1,002.47		$0.4118	$2.47
8	$1,002.88		$0.4120	$2.88
9	$1,003.29		$0.4121	$3.29
10	$1,003.70		$0.4123	$3.70
11	$1,004.12		$0.4125	$4.12
12	$1,004.53		$0.4127	$4.53
13	$1,004.94		$0.4128	$4.94
14	$1,005.36		$0.4130	$5.36
15	$1,005.77		$0.4132	$5.77
16	$1,006.18		$0.4133	$6.18
17	$1,006.60		$0.4135	$6.60
18	$1,007.01		$0.4137	$7.01
19	$1,007.42		$0.4138	$7.42
20	$1,007.84		$0.4140	$7.84
21	$1,008.25		$0.4142	$8.25
22	$1,008.67		$0.4143	$8.67
23	$1,009.08		$0.4145	$9.08
24	$1,009.49		$0.4147	$9.49
25	$1,009.91		$0.4149	$9.91
26	$1,010.32		$0.4150	$10.32
27	$1,010.74		$0.4152	$10.74
28	$1,011.16		$0.4154	$11.16
29	$1,011.57		$0.4155	$11.57
30	$986.99	$25.00	$0.4157	$11.99*

Now, let's look at credit card B. Say you received a 26% interest rate because you were late with a payment, and we've learned that interest builds each day. At the end of the month, you've racked up almost $21 in interest charges. Just making the monthly minimum payment of $25 will take more than seven-and-a-half years to pay off the balance and cost you $1,350 in interest. However, if you double your payment to $50 per month, the whole situation changes. You would pay off your credit card in just over two years and save more than $1,000 in interest costs.

(** These examples assume no additional purchases were made.*)

So, it is imperative that you remember to pay your credit card bills on time, and pay more than the monthly minimum. If you pay just the minimum, additional charges can make the problem (your financial situation) seem unbeatable.

TYPES OF CREDIT CARDS

There are two main types of credit cards: unsecured and secured.

Unsecured Cards

Unsecured cards are the most popular credit cards. They don't require you to have any collateral. Credit is issued based upon your credit worthiness. Lenders will look at factors such as your credit score and income when determining how much credit to grant you. If you decide to get an unsecured card, start with a low credit limit like $500. Again, try to pay off your charges in full each month to avoid interest charges.

If you're unable to pay off the balance each month, make a plan to clear it within a certain time frame. Say you charge a $300 MP3 player and can only afford about $60 a month. That means you'd be able to pay it off in about five months. Remember: you'll be paying interest, so you'll end up paying back more than $300. So be careful; do you really "need" that MP3 player, or would you rather pay the bank for a part of it?

Secured Cards

Secured cards typically require you to back up your credit limit with a savings account. For example, a $500 limit would

Credit card B charges 26% interest and has monthly minimum payment of $25

Day	Balance	Payment	Daily Interest	Cumulative Interest
1	$1,000.00			
2	$1,000.71		$ 0.7123	$0.71
3	$1,001.43		$ 0.7128	$1.43
4	$1,002.14		$ 0.7133	$2.14
5	$1,002.85		$ 0.7139	$2.85
6	$1,003.57		$ 0.7144	$3.57
7	$1,004.28		$ 0.7149	$4.28
8	$1,005.00		$ 0.7154	$5.00
9	$1,005.71		$ 0.7159	$5.71
10	$1,006.43		$ 0.7164	$6.43
11	$1,007.15		$ 0.7169	$7.15
12	$1,007.86		$ 0.7174	$7.86
13	$1,008.58		$ 0.7179	$8.58
14	$1,009.30		$ 0.7184	$9.30
15	$1,010.02		$ 0.7190	$10.02
16	$1,010.74		$ 0.7195	$10.74
17	$1,011.46		$ 0.7200	$11.46
18	$1,012.18		$ 0.7205	$12.18
19	$1,012.90		$ 0.7210	$12.90
20	$1,013.62		$ 0.7215	$13.62
21	$1,014.34		$ 0.7220	$14.34
22	$1,015.07		$ 0.7225	$15.07
23	$1,015.79		$ 0.7231	$15.79
24	$1,016.51		$ 0.7236	$16.51
25	$1,017.24		$ 0.7241	$17.24
26	$1,017.96		$ 0.7246	$17.96
27	$1,018.69		$ 0.7251	$18.69
28	$1,019.41		$ 0.7256	$19.41
29	$1,020.14		$ 0.7262	$20.14
30	$995.86	$25.00	$ 0.7267	$20.86*

require maintaining a balance of $500 in your savings account. You would have to deposit more money into your savings account to increase your available credit. For those wishing to get their first credit card, a secured card is a wise choice. If the bill isn't paid, the bank will withdraw money from your savings account to pay the balance. This will help you learn to charge only what you can reasonably expect to pay back, thereby avoiding financial disaster. Secured credit cards also serve as a good stepping-stone to obtaining unsecured cards.

Debit Cards (also known as "check cards")

Although debit cards are not credit cards, they carry the Visa or MasterCard logo and allow you to make purchases, from which the cost is automatically deducted from your checking account. For many, check cards are more convenient than carrying a checkbook and are simply easier to use. When making purchases, you don't have to worry about wasting time looking for a pen or filling out your check.

If the transaction is processed as a debit, all you have to do is enter your personal identification number (PIN). Debit cards can be used for Internet purchases, as well. Most retail stores will allow you to get cash back on top of your purchase, so you can make a withdrawal from your account without the hassle of finding an ATM. Furthermore, this can help avoid the convenience fees that financial institutions charge for using ATMs that aren't owned by your bank.

Also, because Visa and MasterCard are accepted worldwide, debit cards bearing those logos are usually accepted globally. They are a good option when you are learning to manage credit because no debt is involved. Additionally, they are not as restrictive as secured cards, which require maintaining a savings account with withdrawal limitations. One drawback to consider is that debit cards will not help you establish a credit history because how you use them is not reported to credit reporting agencies.

ADDITIONAL CREDIT CARD COSTS

Over-limit fees

Credit card companies will charge if you exceed your credit limit. It's extremely important to try to keep your credit balance manageable because it's not uncommon to be charged fees in excess of $35 for each billing period that you go over your credit limit. This will increase your monthly bill. For example, if your scheduled payment is $25, the late fee charges will be tacked on to that total, increasing the amount to $60. For those who are already strapped for cash, over-limit fees can cause further setbacks in managing finances.

Credit Card Insurance

If you read the fine print in credit card offers, you are likely familiar with payment protection plans or credit insurance. These offers promise to protect your credit rating in the event you die or become disabled or unemployed. In most cases these benefits will last for a set period of time, such as six months to a year. However, it's important to know that there are different types of coverage, such as:

Involuntary unemployment – The insurer makes your credit card payment if you are laid off or fired from your job. However, it will not pay if you decide to quit your job voluntarily.

Hospitalization – If you are hospitalized for more than two nights in a given month, this insurance will typically cover your credit card payment for that month.

Disability – This type of coverage will pay your credit card payment if you become medically disabled.

Credit insurance is often not as cost-effective as taking out life insurance or disability insurance. If you have multiple credit cards, you would end up taking out several credit insurance policies, which can be very expensive. If you have a $10,000 balance on your credit cards and the cost for insurance is $0.80 per $100 in charges, the monthly payment for coverage would be $80 per month. And it gets worse – as your credit card balance goes up, your cost for the insurance will rise, as well! Many jobs provide employees with life insurance and disability insurance coverage at no cost or at discounted rates, so think twice before signing up for credit insurance. If you do sign up and later change your mind, remember – you can cancel these policies at any time. Check Chapter 13 for more information on other types of insurance.

OTHER TYPES OF CREDIT

Credit cards represent just one area you'll need to navigate on your path to financial freedom. Here are some others:

Installment Credit

Mortgages and car loans are examples of installment credit. These types of loans require you to make fixed payments over a specific time period.

Similar to a secured credit card, which uses your savings account as a backup, your home or vehicle is pledged as collateral. If you fail to pay, the lender can take away your property through foreclosure. Your credit score will also plummet, making it harder to obtain credit in the future.

Service Bills

When you think about credit, you may not consider utility and cell phone bills. But that's what they are: agreements that you will pay for a specified service to receive some type of benefit. For example, if you have a gym membership, you have to pay the monthly bill to have the right to use the facility. In many cases, failing to pay service bills on time will result in late payments being noted and tacked on to your credit report.

Line of Credit

A line of credit is similar to a credit card because you will only receive a bill if you use it. There are two main lines of credit for consumers: home equity and signature.

Home equity lines are secured by your residence. The credit available to you is determined by the amount of equity in your home. If, for example, your home is worth $150,000 and your mortgage balance is $100,000, the equity is $50,000 ($150,000 - $100,000 = $50,000). If the balance of your line of credit is not paid, the lender can foreclose on the property.

A signature line of credit is unsecured and carries a higher interest rate than home equity lines because they aren't backed by collateral like a house. Lenders grant signature lines based on your credit history. People use them for a variety of reasons, such as for home improvements and paying off other bills. Also, if you have unexpected expenses and no cash, lines of credit can be very helpful because they usually carry lower interest rates than cash advances from your credit card.

A word of caution: I would not suggest using a home equity line to consolidate bills such as car payments and credit card purchases. The interest rates and monthly payments are lower than some other credit and loan options, but you put your home at risk if you can't pay the bill.

Just as when shopping for credit cards, take the time to consider the benefits and risks of using a line of credit. If you decide the pluses outweigh the minuses, then look for the best terms. Just be sure to stop all optional spending until your debt is paid.

Student Loans

When I graduated from college, I had no job and owed $8,000 from student loans. I felt overwhelmed because I didn't know how I was going to pay that debt along with all of my other bills. Fortunately, I had a six-month grace period before any payments were due. Before that term ended, I called my lender and explained my situation. My loan was placed in forbearance for three months. The good news was, I didn't have to make any payments during that 90-day period. The bad news, of course, was that interest accrued, so the total cost of my loan went up.

It helps to know what types of student loans are available and what the terms are. There are basically two types of student loans:

Subsidized – These are need-based loans. The government pays the interest while you are in school (provided you are enrolled at least on a part-time basis).

Unsubsidized – These are non-need based. You, not the government, are responsible for the interest on the loan as soon as you receive the check. I knew people in college who borrowed more than they needed. Where else can you get a loan to live a nice lifestyle that doesn't require a credit check? Remember, even though you don't have to pay back your student loans while you are enrolled at least part-time, you will have to pay at some point in the future.

Repayment Options

Equal Payment – This means you pay the principal and interest on your loans. The payments are fixed for the life of the loan.

Graduated Payment –These payments start low but increase at regular intervals; usually every two years. In the early years of the loan you'll pay mostly interest, but over time, as your payment goes up, a bigger portion will go toward paying the principal.

Income-sensitive – In this case, your payment is based on a percentage of your income. The amount can range from as low as 4% of your salary to as much as 25%. As with graduated loans, this option offers lower payment amounts to ease your transition to the workforce, but it increases the overall costs because more interest accumulates before the loan is paid in full.

Consolidation

Consolidation is another way to lower your monthly student loan payments. If you have several loans or want to lock in on a certain interest rate, consolidating your loans can create a more manageable bill.

Here's how it works: The lender will issue a check to pay for all of your student loans. It then creates a new loan for you with a new repayment schedule. These loans can be spread out over twenty-five years.

Loan Tips

Before skipping a payment on your student loan, talk with your lender to determine if it will offer a repayment plan that fits your budget. This is very important, because failing to pay your bill on time will be noted on your credit report. Some lenders will offer a reduction in your interest rate or cash and rewards for paying your bill on time over a specified time period (usually at least twenty-four consecutive months).

I know how tough it is to pay bills right out of college, but it's important to develop your own repayment plan that pays more than your lender requires. Ideally, you want to pay more than the monthly minimum payment to cut down on your repayment period and lower your interest costs.

Think about it this way: If you have a student loan with a $25,000 balance, a 6% annual interest rate and a minimum payment of $245, it would take twelve years to pay off your debt. However, if you increase your payment to $300 per month, it will knock three years off your schedule and free up your money for other things.

TYPES OF CREDIT TO AVOID

Next, we will explore payday, auto title, and refund anticipation loans. Put simply, we're going to play Devil's advocate here: the best advice is, don't use them! But if you have no other option, consider them as short-term loans that you need to repay within one month. Because the fees are high, you should not consider these loans if you can't pay them off within one month.

Payday Loans

You've probably seen the advertisements either on TV or in spam email for loans to help you make it until payday. These are short-term loans with very high interest rates. These companies prey on people who are struggling financially or have credit problems. As long as you have a steady paycheck and a checking account, you can get a payday loan.

Here's how it works: You fill out an application with your contact information. You tell the company how much you want to borrow. (These companies typically lend up to $500.) Next, you give the company a post-dated check or authorization to debit your account. You then receive your much-needed cash minus the fees (which range from $15 to $30 per $100 borrowed).

Now, let's think about this: A $15 fee per $100 borrowed translates into an APR of almost 400%. So if you borrow $300, you may pay $45 in fees to borrow $255. When payday arrives, your check is cashed to satisfy the loan. Because most of the borrowers really can't afford to pay the loan, they get a new one from the lender and pay the fee again.

If the loan is extended for eight pay periods, you will have paid for the loan twice ($615 = $255 + $315 in fees {45 * 8}).

In the event you lack the cash in your account to cover the post-dated check the lender is holding, you risk having your check bounce. This will cause even more fees, because the bank and the payday lender will charge you for having insufficient funds and may threaten to take legal action.

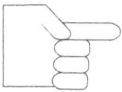

Consider these facts carefully, cited from the Center for Responsible Lending:

- *Five million payday borrowers fall into this debt trap each year.*
- *Ninety-one percent of all payday loans are made to borrowers with five or more payday loans.*
- *On average, borrowers receive eight to thirteen payday loans per year.*

Below is an email I received to lure me into displaying an ad on my Web site to encourage people to apply for payday loans:

"A payday loan is the fastest way to get cash online for emergency expenses. Applying and qualifying for a payday loan is quick and easy, and there are no documents to fax. Your visitors will love the opportunity to get up to $1,500 to their bank accounts the same business day, absolutely hassle-free."

Auto Title Loans

Auto title loans are short-term loans, typically for thirty days or fewer. If you own your vehicle, you could use it to obtain this type of loan. Auto title loan companies don't bother to check your credit because they require you to provide a set of keys, which they will use to repossess your vehicle if you default on the loan. Loan amounts are determined by the fair market value of your car, but are far less than the vehicle's worth. You can go to the Kelley Blue Book website (www.kbb.com) to get an estimate of your vehicle's worth.

Loan amounts are usually at least $600, but no more than $2,500. The interest rate on the loan could be 30%, but that rate is for one month. So, if you have a $500 loan, the interest would be $150 ($500 * 30%). You would therefore owe $650 at the end of the month.

If you can't pay the full amount, the lender will roll the loan over to the next month. So, if you are only able to pay the $150 in interest, the next month you will owe $650 on top of the money you already paid because the interest is continuing to increase at a rate of 30% each month.

Refund Anticipation Loans

As tax season approaches each year, we all start to hear the ads on television and radio funded by tax preparers and car dealers who promise to deliver your refund the same day. What these companies are really offering are loans. These outfits essentially give you an advance against your refund, but it comes at a cost – and a very steep one, at that. Fees for the loan and preparation of tax forms can start at $100 and exceed $200 in some cases. It may seem like a small price to pay to get your funds quickly, but that is money that could have helped pay down a credit card bill or some other debt in the meantime. Many online tax preparation companies are part of the IRS's Free File program, which allows consumers to file their tax returns electronically for free if you meet certain requirements. Check http://www.irs.gov for more details. Now that the IRS has become more efficient at processing electronic returns, you can get your refund between eight to fifteen days. So avoid these expensive loans and be patient so you can receive all of your hard-earned money.

Payday, auto title, and refund anticipation loans underscore even more the need to develop a budget and build up an emergency fund to "cushion" you in the event you are ever short on cash (and because this is life, you will be, at one time or another)! If you don't have any cash left after paying your bills, you need to adjust your spending habits so you can build up enough savings to avoid falling into these traps.

Here are some tips from the Consumer Federation of America on handling cash crunches without borrowing:

- Before you are late on a rent, mortgage, or utility payment, speak with the creditor. For non-interest bills, such as utility or telephone bills, ask about making payment arrangements. Ask to delay payment until your paycheck arrives or set up a repayment schedule that stretches out payments. Make sure to ask about fees or extra costs for extended payments.
- Delay purchasing expensive items until you have cash. If a car repair is causing the cash-flow problem, explore public transportation options until you have the funds together to repair your vehicle. See if any co-workers live nearby so that you can car-pool to work.
- Apply for assistance programs, such as emergency utility funds. Take advantage of local charity, religious, or community programs that help families make ends meet in a crisis.
- Work overtime or pick up extra work to bring in more income. Sell something of value that you no longer need.
- Consider adjusting the amount withheld for taxes to provide more money in your paycheck instead of over-withholding every payday to get a big tax refund later.

Things to Remember

1. If you use a credit card, remember that the amount you owe is a loan and must be repaid. If you don't pay the bill on time, you can damage your credit history, thus making it tougher to get credit in the future.

2. If you are just starting out, try an unsecured credit card with a low limit ($500 or less). This gives you a chance to try things out to determine whether you are ready to handle a higher limit in the future.

3. Secured cards require a savings account, which serves as your credit limit and becomes collateral if you fail to pay your bill on time.

4. Shop around for the card that best meets your needs.

5. Avoid payday, auto title and refund anticipation loans. If you need cash and don't have an emergency fund, consider using a line of credit to help your short-term needs. Then create a plan to pay it off as soon as possible.

CHAPTER 4
BREAKING DOWN CREDIT REPORTS

What's the lowdown on credit reports?
What's everybody talking about, and why does it
seem to be such a big deal? Why do they matter?

Well, if you've ever had a credit card application declined, you already know. They can create – or crush – a chance to obtain credit.

Each month, your payment history is shared with major reporting companies such as Experian, Equifax and TransUnion. Do you pay on time? Are you repeatedly late? All of this information gets logged on your report. And here's another reason to care: The positives and the missteps stay on your report for years.

HERE ARE THE MAJOR SECTIONS OF A CREDIT REPORT:

Personal Information

This segment details identifying information such as your name, address and Social Security number. It also lists your current and past employers.

Account Information

This is the part where, if you've managed credit well, looking at your record should make you proud. If you've stumbled, get ready for a jolt. Everything is here -- the accounts you pay on time, the bills you blow off, the accounts you closed or forgot you had. You'll find information on your car loans, mortgages, credit cards, student loans and other types of loans. Each account shows the amount of your credit line, payment history, and how much you owe.

Public Records

If you owe the government money, you'll certainly find that listed here. Items such as a tax lien on your house or late child-support payments are noted in this section.

Inquiries

Two types of inquiries appear on credit reports. One kind is made by potential creditors. When you receive mail offers of pre-approved credit cards, that means a company has looked at your credit report before contacting you. You make the other type of inquiry, which is more important. Each time you apply for credit, it is noted on your report. Creditors will consider this information in determining whether to grant credit to you. Be careful how often you apply for credit cards. A lender may be alarmed if you open several accounts in a short time frame.

As you can see from the chart above, late payments remain on your credit report for several years. The clock starts from the date of your last payment (also known as the "date of last

How long will information remain on your credit report?	
Open account in good standing	Indefinitely
Late or missed payment	7 years
Collection accounts	7 years
Chapter 7 bankruptcy	10 years
Chapter 13 bankruptcy	7 years
Unpaid tax liens	15 years
Paid tax lien	7 years
Credit inquiries	2 years
Source: Experian	

activity") that led to the account being turned over to a collection agency. Typically, after about 120 days, a bill will be sent to a collections agency.

For example, if you missed your credit card payment in January 2009, the account would have gone into collection in April, but your date of last activity was January. Therefore, it will be January 2016 before that account will be removed from your credit report.

Credit Scores

Credit reporting companies use complex formulas to decide credit scores. The purpose of these tallies is to figure out how much risk you pose as a customer. Only objective information such as your payment history and credit usage is used in the calculation. Factors like your race, age, religion or place of employment are not considered. Lenders use your credit risk score, sometimes individually and sometimes in conjunction with your credit report, to help determine the likelihood that you will pay your bill on time if you are approved for credit.

Each company has a different model for calculating scores, but they all take into account five factors: promptness of payment, ratio of credit used to total available credit, length of credit history, types of credit used, and the number of recent credit inquiries. Your credit score is not a part of your credit report. If you want to know what it is, you must purchase it separately.

The FICO score is the most popular in the United States. It was developed by Fair Isaac Corp. to assist lenders in making decisions about granting credit; however, it is not the only credit risk score. All of the major credit bureaus have their own scoring systems.

Credit risk scores are not static. A mark of 750 (generally considered very good) can easily fall to the lower 500s (generally regarded poor) if bills are not paid on time, so try not to get hung up on your credit score number. It's more important to understand your risk factors, which are outlined here, in order of importance:

1. **Payment history.** Missed payments will hurt your credit report more than any other factor.
2. **Debt load.** Say you have a $4,000 balance on a credit card with a $5,000 limit and three other cards with an

additional $15,000 in available credit. You are using only 20% of your existing credit limit ($4,000/$20,000). The model would give you a higher score than someone who has only one card with a $4,000 balance on a $5,000 limit. Even though you have a high balance on one card, you have used a much smaller percentage of your total available credit. The person who has only $5,000 in available credit has used 80% of his or her existing credit ($4,000/$5,000). Because the scoring models work like this, keep cards in good standing open – even if you have no balance.

3. **Types of accounts.** Lenders like to see customers who can handle different types of credit (e.g., credit cards, car loans, mortgage loans). Your payment history on credit cards is the most important because unlike automobile and mortgage loans, which carry the same payment amount each month, credit card payments change based on your usage. If you can manage multiple types of accounts and pay all those bills on time, it shows that you know how to manage your credit, and it will increase your score.

4. **Inquiries.** Opening too many accounts in a short period of time will have a negative impact on your credit report. If you are planning to buy a house or car in two or three months, don't open several new accounts right before that time because it will lower your score.

You can get a free estimate of your FICO score at www.bankrate.com/brm/fico/calc.asp. This site will give a range of where your score may fall. Another Web site that has useful information is www.nationalscoreindex.com. This site is sponsored by Experian and will allow you to check the average Experian score by a particular state, region, or zip code. It also lists the average debt load, credit inquiries, percentage of credit used to available credit, and late payments.

It's important to remember that lenders use different credit scoring models when determining whether to grant credit. A credit score you access for a fee from the Internet may be totally different from the score a lender is examining when you apply for a loan. Car insurance companies will look at a model that gives more weight to your past claims. If you are applying for a car loan, the lender will focus more on your past automobile payment history.

In the past, lenders used a paper-and-pencil formula to determine whether to grant credit. If you had a short credit history, you might have been rejected because there wasn't enough data to assess. The benefit of credit risk scoring models is that they strike a balance between negative factors, such as a brief credit history, and positive factors, like paying your bills on time, to generate a score regardless of the length of your credit history.

Disputes

Sometimes even credit bureaus get it wrong. Check your report at least annually to make sure the information about you is correct. If you find an error, write a letter or send an email to the credit agencies to dispute the information. Include any documents that back up your claim. Once a dispute request is made, the bureau will contact the lender to verify the information you are challenging. If the lender doesn't respond or produce evidence that a bill belongs to you within thirty days, it will be removed from your credit report. If personal information is incorrect, it will be updated immediately. Correct information will stay on your report. Be diligent in following up with these agencies to make sure your credit report reflects accurate information. Remember, it will follow you the rest of your life.

Some services claim to legally remove information from your credit report by sending several letters disputing an account in the hope that the creditor will fail to respond within thirty days and the account will be deleted. Don't waste your money. These scams are illegal.

By law, you are entitled to receive one free report each year. Request copies from all three agencies. Some accounts may only appear on one bureau's report. For a fee, these companies also offer products to monitor your credit report more often.

Another place you can go for a copy of your report is www.annualcreditreport.com. This centralized source allows you to receive a copy of each of your credit reports from the three bureaus.

The three major credit reporting agencies:

Equifax   (800) 685-1111   www.equifax.com

Experian   (888) 397-3742   www.experian.com

Trans Union (800) 888-4213   www.transunion.com

Of course by law you're entitled to know your credit history and current status, and you certainly have free access to it once a year, as you well should, but why should you want this information? Why is it important? Some people don't even know these companies exist, and still others do, but they don't care and thus don't even exercise their rights to their own financial information!

It's important because like any other company, people are involved, and when people are involved, mistakes can be made. So, it's just a good idea to do a yearly "check and see" to verify all your personal information, make sure it is up to date, and especially cast a keen eye over this material to make certain that the accounts listed on the report are indeed yours.

For example, my brother was named after my dad, and there was a situation one year in which some of my brother's debts showed up on my dad's credit report. Thankfully, this problem was fixed after the creditor noticed they had different Social Security numbers. This was a "good mistake," so to speak, and it was caught fairly early on, so no real damage was done. But something that goes unchecked for years can add up to one whopper of a financial quandary one day if you don't check your credit reports at least once a year. It's like having insurance on your personal financial information – don't go without it.

UNIVERSAL DEFAULT

We've discussed how closely banks and credit unions will monitor your accounts and snag you with late fees the moment it turns midnight and you don't have enough cash in your account to cover a check that just posted that very minute. So you probably think your credit card company doesn't really care if you are late on your car payment as long as their payment arrives on time. After all, you don't drive up to a "branch" credit card company; they're off somewhere in headquarters, right?

Well, back up and think again, because "Big Brother" is here to stay, and believe me, he's watching to make sure you pay all of your bills on time. Many credit card companies use a policy known as universal default. Unlike a basic default, which allows a creditor to increase your interest rate if you pay your bill late, universal default allows creditors the right to charge penalties for failing to pay other creditors on time.

Here's how it works: Say you're late on your car payment. A credit card company that adheres to universal default could then increase the interest rate on your credit card – even though those two bills are from different sources. According to Consumer Action, other financial missteps that can trigger universal default include:

- Going over your available credit limit
- Bouncing a check for payment
- Using too much of your available credit limit
- A drop in credit score

In the past, lenders would look at consumer credit reports to determine whether someone qualified for credit line increases or special offers, like reduced interest rates. But times have changed – now, they also look at your payment history with other accounts. That's why it's important to read the fine print in credit card disclosure statements to make sure you understand what you are getting into before accepting that new card.

Here are some examples of statements that reflect universal default:

> *"We may change the rates, fees, and terms of your account at any time for any reason. These reasons may be based on information in your credit report, such as your failure to make payments to another creditor when due, amounts owed to other creditors, the number of credit accounts outstanding, or the number of credit inquiries."*

"We may change the terms based on information such as other credit card accounts you have and their balances."

"If you fail to make payments on time or if we in good faith reasonably believe that the prospect of payment to us or any other creditor is impaired, we reserve the right to increase your APR to the default rate."

See how easy it is to fall behind, and how quickly this can happen? Just one late payment can cause other creditors to boost your interest rate because many share credit information. What's even worse is that some companies don't let their customers know that universal default has been triggered until they receive a bill with the new interest rate.

Tips to Avoid Universal Default

➤ Pay all your bills on time. Many banks offer online bill-pay for free. You can set up this service to remind you when bills are due. Sometimes that little nudge is all we need to remember to pay bills in a timely manner.

➤ Read the fine print. It's important to read credit card disclosure statements to understand how the terms of your account can be changed. If you see wording similar to, "We reserve the right to change the terms of this agreement at any time and for any reason," you have a card with universal default.

➤ Transfer balances to cards without universal default clauses. Don't overextend yourself with credit. Try to keep your balances less than 50% of your available credit limit. Universal default can trigger default of other creditors if you are maintaining high credit balances.

➤ Monitor your credit reports regularly. The major credit bureaus provided above offer services that can issue updates on your credit report. If you plan to dispute a late payment on your credit report, do it right away. This is your money; that means it's serious business.

Credit Card Accountability, Responsibility and Disclosure Act of 2009

In May 2009, legislation was passed to allow for better consumer disclosures as it relates to Universal Default and other bad practices of the credit card industry. Credit card companies can retroactively increase your interest rate for late payments, but now you have to be two months behind on your bill. They can also no longer punish cardholders for being late on unrelated bills. After this bill is enacted in February 2010, if you have paid your bill on time for six months after a sixty-day delinquency, the credit card company has to restore you to the rate before the increase. Companies can still increase your interest rate with this new law, but they have to give you forty-five days' written notice. There are also fee restrictions to protect consumers. In the past, credit card companies would allow charges over the credit limit to go through so they could charge extra fees, but now consumers will not have to pay these fees if they don't elect to have the creditor approve purchases that exceed the limit.

NOTES

Things to Remember

1. Pay bills on time. One thirty-day late payment can have a very damaging effect on your report.

2. Use credit sensibly. Try to keep balances below 50% of your available limit.

3. Leave accounts in good standing open. These records stay on your credit report indefinitely and help improve your score.

4. Limit credit inquiries. It's OK to check your credit report periodically, but don't apply for new credit too often in a short time frame.

CHAPTER 5

Navigating Through Credit Problems

*Many people have problems paying bills
on time at some point in their lives.*

I know I've certainly had my share of cash crunches, which prompted me to write this book so others wouldn't fall into the same traps. But I always found a way to bounce back, and so can you. If you are in a situation where you can't make your credit card payments, start by talking to the card issuer. Though this move might seem a bit "backwards," the truth is, it's always best to honor your commitments to your credit card companies and alert them as soon as you feel you may be slipping behind. If you take this proactive step forward, you'll find that most credit card companies will be willing to work with you. They would rather receive something than nothing, and making a payment arrangement can preserve your credit rating. They also don't want to have to put your account into collections, which is a hassle for both you and the company. So it truly will behoove you to be upfront and honest with your creditors about your financial situation. They certainly understand that everyone gets in a jam at some time or another, and they will appreciate your gesture.

You see, each time you are late with credit payments, the issuer makes a note on your credit report. Notations are made for thirty, sixty, ninety, and one-hundred-twenty days past due.

Each new mark hurts your credit score and also makes it more difficult for you to obtain credit for major purchases such as a car or house. In this chapter, we'll discuss some strategies for overcoming credit troubles.

CHARGE OFFS

As we covered in Chapter 4, accounts are turned over to collection agencies after a bill has been late for four months. Charge offs occur when a bill has not been paid for six months. Sometimes payments are overdue because the customer has died or filed for bankruptcy. Whatever the case, if a bill is in the charge-off state, it means that for accounting purposes, the credit card company has written off the debt, but it does not mean it has given up collecting on the debt. Charge offs stay on your report for seven years from the last date of activity. If left unresolved, these situations will absolutely ruin your credit.

When your account is with a collection agency, expect calls and/or letters demanding payment of your debt. If you'd like to negotiate a settlement, by all means call the creditor and work out the details. It's best if the creditor will agree to delete your debt once you pay the agreed-upon amount because that means all of those late payment notations will be removed as well. Also, ask for a letter outlining the agreement before sending any money.

Some people will avoid collections agencies like the plague and literally refuse to pay anything, waiting for those seven years to pass, because by law, certain bad debts will disappear from your credit report after that amount of time. But if you plan to buy a house or car, having several charge offs can cause you to be rejected or receive a high interest rate because it "brands" you as a high-risk customer -- someone who does not pay the bills on time.

CREDIT COUNSELORS

Some people turn to credit counselors for help when their debt becomes unbearable. These organizations will review your bills and assist you in consolidating them into one payment, often with a much-lower interest rate than your individual credit cards. Creditors often fund credit counseling programs because it protects their interests. Again, lenders would rather work with counselors, even if it means accepting lower payments, than be paid nothing. Some people seek credit counseling as a viable way of avoiding bankruptcy.

To find a reputable credit counselor, check the National Foundation for Credit Counseling (http:// www.nfcc.org). This organization sets standards for credit counseling companies and requires them to undergo accreditation every four years. In addition, it maintains a certification process for credit counselors to ensure that they are providing sound financial education while upholding ethical standards.

CREDIT REPAIR SCAMS

"Eradicate card payments and see zero balances. Cancel debts and never make another payment!"

"Discharge debts quickly, painlessly, legally. For the rest of the story about canceling debt, go to our elimination page."

These are excerpts from typical bogus emails I received. Sound familiar to you, too? If you receive any of these types of notes or hear ads on the radio or TV making such claims, remember the old saying: *"If it sounds too good to be true, it probably is."*

Beware of firms that promise the world. For a fee (this being the key phrase), some companies claim to erase bankruptcies and other bad credit. They prey on those who are uneducated or unaware about the legalities of personal financial information. There is absolutely no legal way to remove accurate information on a credit report. If there is an error, you can request an investigation, but that's a free service. According to the Credit Repair Organizations Act, credit repair firms can not advise you to commit illegal acts like changing one letter in your name to create a new credit file or sending several letters disputing an account you know to be correct in hopes that the creditor will fail to verify the debt within thirty days, thereby deleting the account from your report.

One last point on credit repair firms: They can not charge for a service they promise until they fully deliver. If the company says, for instance, that it will eliminate bad debts from your credit report, you do not have to pay until they have delivered on their claim. Some firms will ask you to pay a monthly fee while they work on repairing your credit file. Again, if you don't know your legal rights in this area, you're vulnerable to some of these scams – they often "cover" themselves fairly well, and it's easy to fall into the traps they set.

Read the following passage carefully – it is a direct excerpt from a disclosure from the Federal Trade Commission that requires credit repair companies to give to customers before doing any work:

"You have a right to dispute inaccurate information in your credit report by contacting the credit bureau directly. However, neither you nor any 'credit repair' company or credit repair organization has the right to have accurate, current, and verifiable information removed from your credit report. The credit bureau must remove accurate, negative information from your report only if it is over 7 years old. Bankruptcy information can be reported for 10 years."

Source: Federal Trade Commission

This basically means one thing: You don't need a middle man! You can do anything a legitimate credit repair organization can do on your own! Since you spent the time charging up the debts, get out there and be the one to tackle the problem. Remember, consistently paying your bills on time is the best way to improve your score.

BANKRUPTCY

According to the American Heritage Dictionary, bankruptcy is a voluntary petition where you are judged to be legally insolvent. This basically means that you lack the money to pay your debts. People file for protection under bankruptcy laws for a number of reasons. Some of the more common ones include credit card debt, job loss, medical bills, divorce, or bad financial management.

Bankruptcy may be your choice, or it may be forced upon you by creditors. It can cause debts to either be eliminated or repaid under the direction of the bankruptcy court.

For individuals, there are two basic types of bankruptcy: Chapter 7 and Chapter 13. Those designations refer to their particular chapters within Title 11 of the United States Code. Chapter 7 is often referred to as "liquidation" because it allows certain debts to be eliminated. In some cases, property may be sold to pay down debts. But some states prohibit the selling of certain assets, such as cars and houses, for Chapter 7 bankruptcy purposes. In states where cars are not exempt, they can either be repossessed or the consumer can continue making the payments.

It's important to understand that bankruptcy doesn't wipe away all debts. Items such as child support, tax obligations, and student loans are typically not forgiven.

Chapter 13 is referred to as "reorganization." This type of bankruptcy allows filers the chance to repay their debts. If you have a debt such as a mortgage payment, Chapter 13 gives you the option of catching up on missed payments by spreading the debt out over a longer period of time. The length of repayment depends on the amount owed.

CHANGES IN BANKRUPTCY LAW

In October 2005, a new law was established that requires individuals to receive a certificate from a credit counselor before filing for bankruptcy. The credit counselor must be approved by the U.S. Trustee Program, which oversees the bankruptcy courts in the United States. With this certificate, consumers will receive counseling on budgeting before and after filing.

There have been changes to Chapter 7 bankruptcy, as well. It's no longer an automatic way to eliminate debts. First, the law exempts certain living expenses, like food and rent or mortgage payments, from a standard formula to determine whether a consumer can afford to pay a portion of unsecured debt like credit card bills. Also, your income will be compared to the state median. If it exceeds that amount, you will not be allowed to file a liquidation bankruptcy.

Finally, these changes may possibly increase attorneys' costs. The new laws require that more data be obtained, and lawyers are required to vouch that the information submitted to the courts is accurate. Therefore, lawyer fees may accelerate. If the courts discover that the information the lawyer reported to the bankruptcy court is false, legal action can be taken against both you and your lawyer.

The purpose of the new laws is to promote good financial management skills. There is an adage that says: "If you give a man a fish, you feed him for a day, but if you teach him how to fish, you feed him for a lifetime." Many people have just never been taught how to properly manage their personal finances, and the government's hope is that this type of counseling will get folks on the right track and help them avoid filing for bankruptcy again in the future.

Keep in mind that bankruptcies can remain on your credit report up to ten years. Situations like family or medical emergencies are sometimes unavoidable as it relates to overextending yourself with credit, try to think carefully before you overcharge. Do you really want to end up waiting ten long years to be able to attain enough credit to buy a house or a car for yourself or your family?

As I mentioned earlier, you can contact creditors directly if you realize that you are going to be unable to make payments on time, and you can set up a repayment schedule on your own without going to credit counselors or filing for bankruptcy.

CHECK CREDIT FOR ERRORS

By law, credit reporting companies have to delete an account from your record seven years after the date of last activity for past due accounts. Remember to check your report to make sure your account information is updated at least once per year.

Things to Remember

1. If you have some negative marks on your credit report like late payments or collection accounts, you can re-establish your credit by opening new accounts. Start with a secured credit card. Make one or two small purchases each month and pay the bill off. Over time, this will improve your credit score.

2. Check your credit report periodically to make sure all the information is accurate.

3. If your credit card bills are so high you can only pay the monthly minimum, go over Chapter 1 again to make sure you understand budgeting or seek the help of a credit counselor who offers classes on developing budgets.

4. Filing for Chapter 7 bankruptcy (liquidation) has gotten tougher. The government is steering more people to Chapter 13 (reorganization), which essentially sets up a payment plan to pay for debts rather than relieving you from paying them back, as with Chapter 7.

CHAPTER 6
AVOIDING IDENTITY THEFT

*Identity theft occurs when someone has access
to your identification information.*

W e all do it: You go through last month's mail and try to clear away some of the clutter, throwing away old bills in the process without a thought. But hold on for a minute: consider what you're doing. Thieves routinely rummage through trash looking for any bit of personal information. Some will pilfer your credit card number. Others will swipe your Social Security and bank account numbers. They will assume your identity, steal and commit fraud in your name.

Identity theft is becoming rampant in America. According to the Consumer Sentinel report published by Federal Trade Commission, the number of complaints was up more than 37% between 2006 and 2008. In 2008, there were more than 640,000 cases of fraud reported, costing consumers more than $1.8 billion.

How do you protect yourself? The first move is to make sure you cut up or shred receipts and bills including details such as your name, address, and account numbers with a cross shredder. This makes it almost impossible for a thief to reassemble the document.

Another safeguard is to check your credit report for errors and signs of suspicious activity. The major credit bureaus, Equifax, Experian, and TransUnion, all have monitoring services that allow users to receive updates on changes that may alert you to identity theft.

According to a report published by the Identity Theft Resource Center, a growing amount of the pilfering is committed among family members. Surprisingly, the most common reported cases are parents using their child's information to obtain credit or services such as phone and utilities. Sadly, many young people are going to be forced to pay for these mistakes by having a bad credit history before they're even old enough to apply for credit themselves.

TYPES OF FRAUD

Financial Identity

If you have credit cards or bank accounts, you could potentially become a victim of financial identity fraud. This occurs when someone tries to either swindle money from your existing accounts or establish new ones in your name. Some criminals will steal your personal checks to purchase goods. These checks will bounce if you don't have enough funds in your account.

Criminals can also use your credit or debit cards to steal from you. In 2001, someone used golfer Tiger Woods' identity – his name and Social Security number -- to pilfer $17,000 worth of merchandise. In 2005, an impostor stole rapper/actor Will Smith's identity and charged nearly $33,000 worth of goods in his name. No one is exempt from this kind of criminal activity. It's a serious and pervasive problem, so always be very, very careful when dispensing with your personal bank statements or any other self-identifying information on paper.

Criminal Identity Theft

Criminal identity theft occurs when a person assumes your identity and violates the law. The imposter may have some type of ID bearing your name and then robs a bank, retail establishment, or commits other crimes. Often, when these criminals are caught, they provide false identification, thereby implicating you. If these are minor crimes like misdemeanors, they can go on your criminal record without your knowledge. However, if the crime is more serious, law enforcement officials can literally take you to jail. Then, you may have to hire a lawyer to help sort everything out. So save yourself the hassle: Get a copy of your criminal report from your local police station periodically to make sure no one has committed crimes using your name.

Protection for Internet Purchases

Because identity theft costs businesses more than $50 billion annually, many jobs have been created for people to work on solutions for reducing losses. CitiGroup now has a free product for its cardholders that allows them to make purchases without providing their actual card numbers. The system generates a random credit card number to make it difficult to steal account information when processing online transactions. Each time you make a purchase on the Internet, a substitute account number is produced, but the purchases are still charged to you and appear on your monthly statement.

Verified by Visa™ is another program designed to protect consumers making online purchases. When shopping at participating retailers, you would enter the usual information, such as your name, address, phone number, and credit card number. Then, a screen appears, prompting you for a password. This is an added level of protection in case your card or number is stolen. The government is also doing its part by imposing stiffer penalties for identity theft cases. Individuals convicted of non-terrorist identity theft will receive two-year prison sentences.

Other Tips to Protect Yourself While Shopping Online

- Buy from merchants with whom you have dealt with in the past and feel you can trust.
- Look for signs of security, such as sites that have https:// or use secure sockets layer (SSL) because they provide an extra layer of protection when entering credit card information.
- Don't share passwords with others. Also try to make them difficult for a hacker to guess by using upper- and lower-case characters as well as numbers and symbols, such as an

underscore (_) or pound sign (#). Also, change your
passwords periodically.

- Make sure you have the latest anti-virus software
  installed on your computer to protect it from malicious
  programs.
- When you complete a transaction, be sure to log off and
  close the browser to ensure that no temporary files are left
  for anyone to peruse.

Skimming

Another form of identity theft that is becoming rampant
around the world is called "skimming." It most commonly
occurs at places where you swipe your debit or credit card, such
ATMs, gas stations and restaurants. At the gas pump, thieves
will strategically attach the skimming device where you swipe
your card. Sometimes it may not be visible to the naked eye or,
if it is, you will more than likely not notice it.

When you swipe your card, the card number is transmitted
twice: once for the merchant and once for the crook. In some
instances a camera may be attached to the device so that the
pilferer can see you enter your pin number while he waits in
his car nearby. This information can then be used to steal
funds from your account to make unauthorized transactions
with your credit card. While some stores demand to see a
driver's license or some other form of photographic
identification when making a purchase to verify your identity,
not all follow that procedure. But stores are beginning to
protect consumers by asking for your zip code after you swipe
the card. Because the thief will likely not know this
information, the purchase will then be denied.

For online transactions, many merchants require the CVV
code, which is a three-digit code on the back of your card. So
far, at least, this information isn't captured by the skimming
device and provides a layer of protection to prevent fraud.

How to protect yourself against skimming:

- ✓ Go inside to pay for gas
- ✓ Never leave your receipt at the credit card center at the gas
  pump or at the ATM. Although it usually doesn't record

your entire account number, you don't want to give any information whatsoever to wandering eyes.

✓ Use online banking to check your transactions on a daily basis.
✓ If skimming does occur, contact both the merchant and your financial institution immediately.

Phishing/Spoof emails

The origin of the word "phishing" comes from the analogy that imposters use email lures to "fish" for personal and account information. "Ph" is a common replacement for "f" by hackers. Phishing emails (also known as spoof emails) are designed to direct you to another website to steal your personal identification or account information to commit fraud.

Phishers use clever tactics by pretending to be well-known companies such as banks and Internet merchants to gain your trust so that you will visit their websites. A few examples of some popular phishing emails are provided below. If you see these or similar ones directing you to another website, do not click on the link within the email. Be sure to read the Internet address. Someone claiming to be a representative of Bank of America might direct you to a site other than its actual address (www.bankofamerica.com).

Tips to Spot Phishing emails

- **Urgent appeals** – These emails may claim that your account will be closed if you fail to confirm your personal information immediately.
- **Request for Security Information** – Occasionally, phishing emails may suggest that your financial institution has lost important information and needs an update.
- **Typos or other errors** – Often, these emails will have spelling or grammatical errors. In addition, there may be a message at the bottom of the email that has nothing to do with the main content.

Sample lines

Below are a few examples of email subject headers that can alert you to a possible phisher:

"Unusual login attempts to your personal account"

"Your account has been violated"

"Important Account Information"

"Valued Customer"

Phone Phishers

Phishers try to lure people on the telephone, too. Some may call you claiming to be employees of credit card companies and ask for the three-digit security code on the back of your card. Even if these scammers have your account number, they may not be able to rack up charges unless they have this code. Merchants use it to verify that the card belongs to you when you make transactions on the Internet or telephone. Only give this sensitive information out to sources you're sure are legitimate. If you are not on the National Do Not Call Registry, sign up at www.donotcall.gov. You can register your home and cell phone numbers.

Email Hoaxes

If you receive an email informing you that you can receive a large monetary award for a small fee or asks you to forward that email on to others, it is most likely a scam. Some of the more common hoaxes are the Nigerian 419, chain letters, and lottery winning emails. Check out the examples below:

Nigerian 419 Scam

This type of email requests your help in moving a large sum of money – part of which the phishers inform you is yours – out of Nigeria or some other country. They will ask that you pay some fees in advance before you can receive your windfall. Think about this for a minute. Why would they just randomly pick you to help in this transaction when the sender knows nothing about you? Here is one version of this type of email:

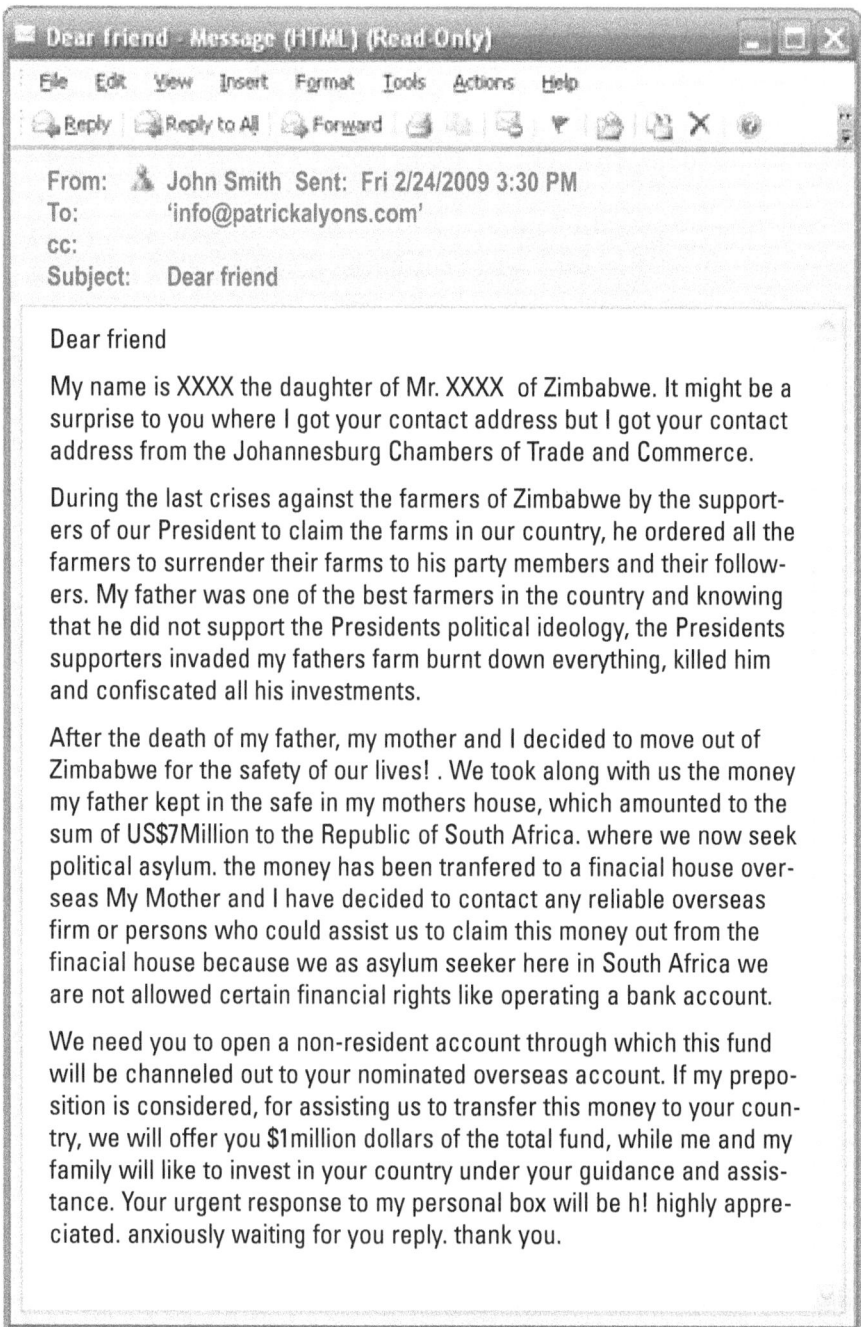

Dear friend - Message (HTML) (Read-Only)

File   Edit   View   Insert   Format   Tools   Actions   Help

Reply   Reply to All   Forward

From: John Smith   Sent: Fri 2/24/2009 3:30 PM
To: 'info@patrickalyons.com'
cc:
Subject: Dear friend

Dear friend

My name is XXXX the daughter of Mr. XXXX of Zimbabwe. It might be a surprise to you where I got your contact address but I got your contact address from the Johannesburg Chambers of Trade and Commerce.

During the last crises against the farmers of Zimbabwe by the supporters of our President to claim the farms in our country, he ordered all the farmers to surrender their farms to his party members and their followers. My father was one of the best farmers in the country and knowing that he did not support the Presidents political ideology, the Presidents supporters invaded my fathers farm burnt down everything, killed him and confiscated all his investments.

After the death of my father, my mother and I decided to move out of Zimbabwe for the safety of our lives! . We took along with us the money my father kept in the safe in my mothers house, which amounted to the sum of US$7Million to the Republic of South Africa. where we now seek political asylum. the money has been tranfered to a finacial house overseas My Mother and I have decided to contact any reliable overseas firm or persons who could assist us to claim this money out from the finacial house because we as asylum seeker here in South Africa we are not allowed certain financial rights like operating a bank account.

We need you to open a non-resident account through which this fund will be channeled out to your nominated overseas account. If my preposition is considered, for assisting us to transfer this money to your country, we will offer you $1million dollars of the total fund, while me and my family will like to invest in your country under your guidance and assistance. Your urgent response to my personal box will be h! highly appreciated. anxiously waiting for you reply. thank you.

Chain Letters

Chain letters will contain information asking you to forward the email to as many people as possible and visit a particular Web site in the hope that someone will fall for the scam and share their personal information. Below is one that I received:

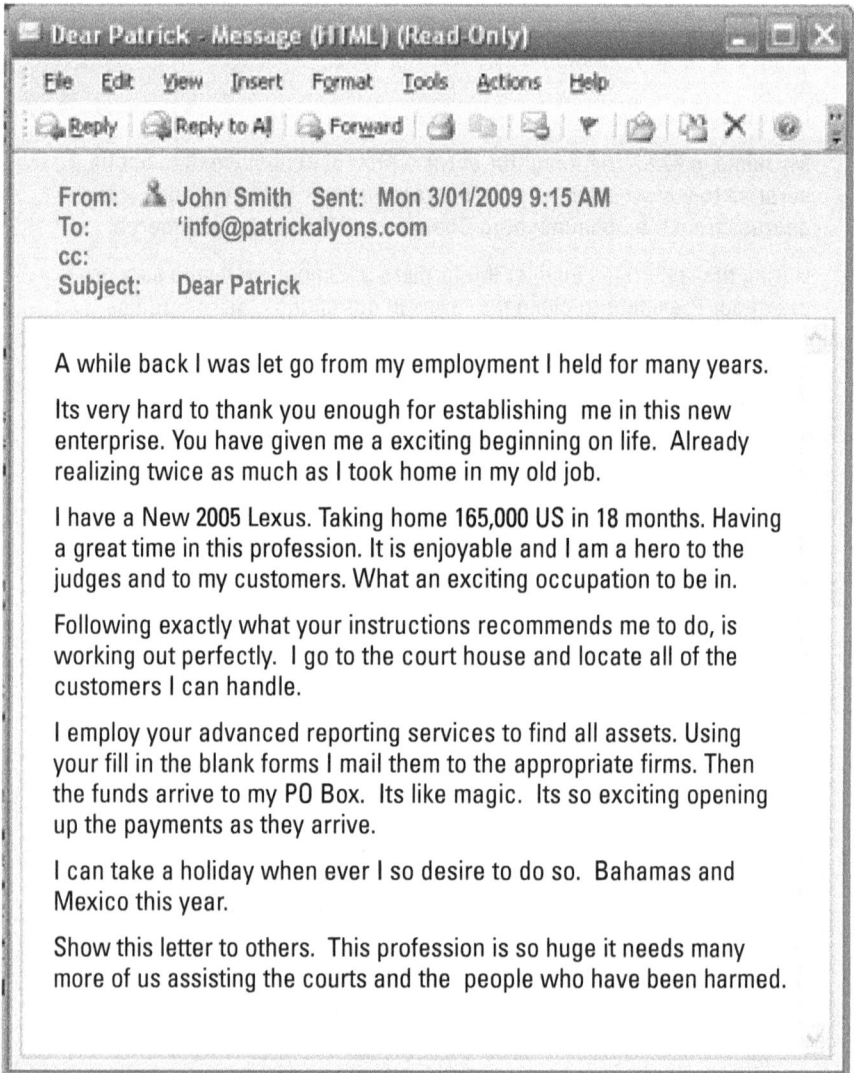

Dear Patrick - Message (HTML) (Read-Only)

File   Edit   View   Insert   Format   Tools   Actions   Help

Reply   Reply to All   Forward

From: John Smith   Sent: Mon 3/01/2009 9:15 AM
To: 'info@patrickalyons.com
cc:
Subject: Dear Patrick

A while back I was let go from my employment I held for many years.

Its very hard to thank you enough for establishing me in this new enterprise. You have given me a exciting beginning on life. Already realizing twice as much as I took home in my old job.

I have a New 2005 Lexus. Taking home 165,000 US in 18 months. Having a great time in this profession. It is enjoyable and I am a hero to the judges and to my customers. What an exciting occupation to be in.

Following exactly what your instructions recommends me to do, is working out perfectly. I go to the court house and locate all of the customers I can handle.

I employ your advanced reporting services to find all assets. Using your fill in the blank forms I mail them to the appropriate firms. Then the funds arrive to my PO Box. Its like magic. Its so exciting opening up the payments as they arrive.

I can take a holiday when ever I so desire to do so. Bahamas and Mexico this year.

Show this letter to others. This profession is so huge it needs many more of us assisting the courts and the people who have been harmed.

Lottery Scams

These emails usually claim that you have won some type of international lottery. The phisher will ask you to send a fee to claim it, so think twice if you receive an email claiming you have won a lottery. Below is one that I received:

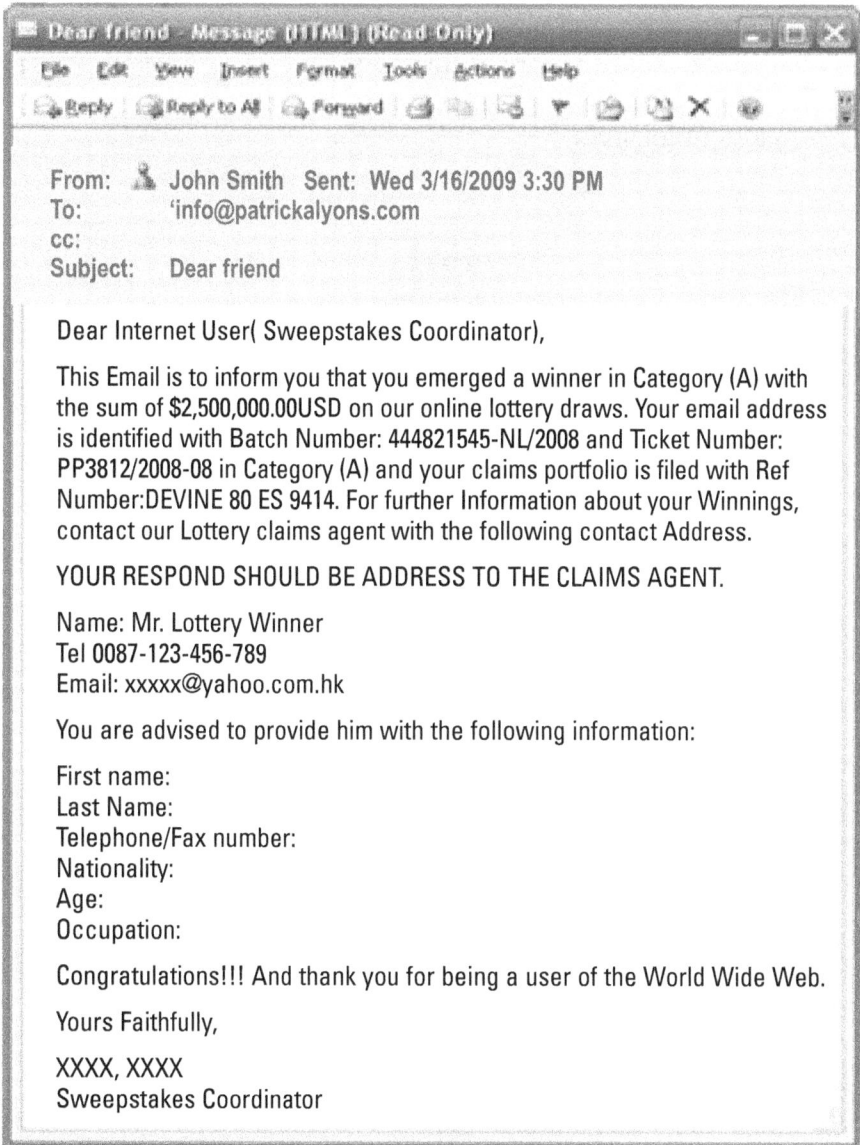

Dear friend - Message (HTML) (Read Only)

File   Edit   View   Insert   Format   Tools   Actions   Help

Reply | Reply to All | Forward

From: John Smith   Sent: Wed 3/16/2009 3:30 PM
To: 'info@patrickalyons.com
cc:
Subject: Dear friend

Dear Internet User(Sweepstakes Coordinator),

This Email is to inform you that you emerged a winner in Category (A) with the sum of $2,500,000.00USD on our online lottery draws. Your email address is identified with Batch Number: 444821545-NL/2008 and Ticket Number: PP3812/2008-08 in Category (A) and your claims portfolio is filed with Ref Number:DEVINE 80 ES 9414. For further Information about your Winnings, contact our Lottery claims agent with the following contact Address.

YOUR RESPOND SHOULD BE ADDRESS TO THE CLAIMS AGENT.

Name: Mr. Lottery Winner
Tel 0087-123-456-789
Email: xxxxx@yahoo.com.hk

You are advised to provide him with the following information:

First name:
Last Name:
Telephone/Fax number:
Nationality:
Age:
Occupation:

Congratulations!!! And thank you for being a user of the World Wide Web.

Yours Faithfully,

XXXX, XXXX
Sweepstakes Coordinator

Money Laundering

You may receive an email containing information that asks you to process a payment, check or money order. The sender will request that you deposit his or her check into your account and forward the money to them electronically. These checks will often bounce, which can cause your bank to charge you fees. Even worse, the perpetrator can implicate you in the crime if he is caught. So please beware of this ripoff.

For more examples, visit www.hoax-slayer.com and www.antiphishing.org.

NOTES

Things to Remember

1. Never give out personal account information by email or over the phone.

2. Do not click on links in unsolicited emails. There is a good chance it is directing you to a website that is collecting personal information.

3. Keep your passwords to yourself and memorize them. When creating your passwords, avoid obvious choices like your name, birthday, pet's name, or the word "password." Do not carry them in your wallet or purse.

4. Never leave receipts at ATMs. Take them home and shred them immediately.

5. When using ATMs, be aware of your surroundings. If you feel wary, cancel your transaction and leave. Try to avoid using ATMs at night because someone could easily sneak up on you.

PART 3

CHAPTER 7

Defining Financial Freedom

*Achieving financial freedom has little
to do with the salary you make.*

Some people bring home $24,000 a year and are free from debt while others earn $150,000 a year and live from paycheck to paycheck. Making more money doesn't always make you happy.

But what can give you peace of mind is having a plan to achieve your financial goals. Use the tools outlined earlier in the book on budgeting and managing credit wisely, create a disciplined savings plan, and find a job you enjoy. In this chapter, we will explore how to discover the right career for you.

FINDING YOUR DREAM JOB

Searching for a job requires a lot of effort. The days of working for one company your whole career are over. Some people may switch jobs once or twice, while others labor their whole life and never find their perfect job. But once you find one that allows you to pursue your passion, the journey becomes worthwhile. Going to work brings fulfillment and peace when you are doing something you enjoy.

Assessing Your Career

Before even starting your job search, determine your interests. One way to do that is by taking a personality test. There are several types you can try. The Keirsey Temperament Sorter II and the Jung-Myers-Briggs Typology Test are among the most popular. Don't let the names scare you. They sound complicated, but they're really simple surveys that can help you learn more about yourself and figure out what career path to choose. You can take the Keirsey Temperament Sorter II for free by visiting www.keirsey.com. There is also a free test based on the Jung-Myers Briggs approach at www.humanmetrics.com.

Creating a Resume

After you zero in on your interests, create a resume to help you get the job you want. List your responsibilities from previous jobs and highlight your achievements. Tell the truth. Lying about qualifications and exaggerating accomplishments can get you fired.

Think of legitimate ways to make your resume stand out. Choose a well-designed style that fits your career choice and personality. Write with strong verbs. Check for typos, spacing and grammatical errors.

You may have heard that resumes have to be just one page long. Some experts say two pages are fine as long as the information is related to the position you're seeking.

Looking for Jobs

The Internet

With the growth of the Internet, looking online for a job has become a cheap and efficient way of finding work. Sites like Monster.com and Careerbuilder.com allow users to post resumes and apply for positions. These sites are both a resource for high school and college students searching for summer jobs and internships and working adults looking for full- and part-time jobs. Unlike snail mail, which can take days to reach employers, a resume posted on the Internet can land on an employer's desk with the click of a button.

Another helpful feature of job Web sites are their resources. Many provide tips to prepare candidates for interviews and give background information on the companies posting jobs. These extras can give you the competitive advantage you need to edge out the competition.

Networking

Networking is simply a "buzzword" for meeting people, exchanging ideas and information, and forging professional and personal connections. You can make formal contacts through professional and trade organizations. These groups often hold meetings or social gatherings where you can interact and exchange business cards. Informal contacts can come from friends, family and neighbors. You can also create these ties by volunteering. You may meet someone who works at the company at which you wish to apply.

When networking, you can ask contacts for direct job leads or for information and advice to help you in your job search. Several companies fill jobs by getting employee referrals, so if there is a place you are interested in, make contact with someone in the department you would like to work. Offer to take that person to lunch or set up a time to go by his or her office to sell your skills. That way, when an opening becomes available, they may very well think of you and give you a call.

Newspapers

Although more employers are listing jobs on the Internet, newspapers are still a good source of job openings. The Sunday paper is a great place to check out listings if you are limiting your search to a specific geographic region.

Conversely, if you want to work in an out-of-town area or even in another state, simply subscribe to that city's Sunday newspaper, and it's nearly as good as being there. Of course the Internet is a faster way to find jobs, but do keep in mind that not all employers list their job openings on the Internet – it's a matter of personal or, shall we say, company, preference. Do not eliminate the newspaper as one of your resources simply because it seems the whole world's attention is fixed on the Internet. You might just assume yourself out of a job!

Companies

Again, some companies prefer to recruit the old-fashioned way rather than opening themselves up to the volume of resumes that may come with posting available jobs on the Internet. But even if a company in which you are interested has no advertised vacancy, you can certainly still send your resume. Then, do a little detective work. Find out the name of the manager in the department you wish to work for and write a letter, asking to schedule an informational interview to highlight your strengths. This type of initiative – and unusual, more forthright style of job searching – can set you apart and may even put you at the top of the list of candidates when a job does become available.

Search Firms

Search firms, also known as headhunters or recruiters, can be a very useful resource for job openings. Companies retain these firms to screen job candidates and narrow the list for interviewees rather than having to pore over hundreds or thousands of resumes themselves to find qualified applicants for certain, specialized jobs. You may apply for a job over the Internet and find that the job was posted by a search firm. Headhunters also network quite heavily to locate good candidates. But remember, the goal of a headhunter is to get you to accept a job. He or she may not care whether it is a good fit for you. Because once you take the job, the headhunter receives a commission, typically paid by the company that hired you.

Thank You!

After interviews, always remember to send thank-you notes. Mail them as soon as possible – certainly within two days of your meeting. Some say it is fine to send an email to thank your interviewer, but I suggest mailing a typed or handwritten note. Because Internet service providers use high-level spam blockers, your thank-you email may not even reach the person if you are not in his or her email address book. Plus, giving a personal touch may set you apart from the competition – in fact, it may go in your employee file one day!

Understanding Employee Benefits

Did you realize that many companies give employees benefits just for coming to work every day? Remember to consider these perks as you evaluate each company's offer. It depends on what you value most, of course, but in some cases, a generous collection of benefits can make a job with a low- to average salary more appealing, just as a stingy package can diminish your interest.

Here are some of the most common benefits employers provide:

Paid Time Off

Paid time off is one of the most common benefits offered by most companies. It can come in the form of vacation time, which can be used at your discretion; sick time; or personal time, which gives you time to handle personal chores. Most companies also give employees various holidays off with pay.

Tuition Reimbursement

Some companies will pay for you to continue your education if it is related to your field of work. These firms typically require you to pay for the cost of tuition and books up front. If you make a passing grade or the grade the company stipulates, they will then reimburse you.

Insurance

In the wide view, insurance is a contract that provides coverage against loss. Policies can be purchased for different contingencies, such as loss of life (life insurance), sickness (health insurance), or long-term illness (disability insurance). Companies often are able to offer these benefits at group rates, which are lower, and plans that are included usually provide more comprehensive benefits than you would be able to get on your own. Another important point is that group plans usually don't require medical exams to obtain a policy like many individual ones do. Some employers will pay your premium, and others may contribute to the cost. Still others will pay nothing at all. It's just all part of the entire package to consider when searching for a job – the company "climate" and whether it fits with your lifestyle.

Health Insurance

This type of insurance helps defray costs if you need to go to the doctor or have other medical needs such as prescription medications. Companies often offer at least two or even three different types of coverage. One option may provide a lower premium, but require you to pay a higher percentage of your medical costs. The two major types of insurance plans are indemnity and managed care:

Indemnity – Also known as a reimbursement plan, indemnity reimburses you for medical expenses regardless of the provider you choose. In most cases, you will receive a percentage of the costs, not the total amount.

Managed care - This plan comes in two varieties: Health Maintenance Organizations (HMOs) and Preferred Provider Organizations (PPOs). With HMOs, you select a primary care physician to handle your health-related needs within a set network of doctors. If you need to see a specialist, your doctor will refer you to one within the group. Under HMOs, if you see a doctor who is not covered by your insurance plan, you will pay a significant part of the charges. PPOs provide more flexibility – you don't have to get referrals from a primary care doctor to see specialists, and they typically have a larger selection of physicians to choose from.

Life Insurance

Life insurance will pay a beneficiary you designate a specific amount of money in the event of your death. More information on life insurance will be covered in Chapter 13.

Disability Insurance

If you become so ill you can't work, how will you pay the bills? Thankfully, many companies offer disability insurance. You can receive short-term disability coverage, which will pay a portion of your wages for a specific time period, usually less than twelve months. For longer-lasting health problems, you can purchase a long-term disability insurance policy.

Retirement

Some companies offer a variety of retirement saving options. The more common types are 401(k), 403(b),. and pension plans, which will be discussed in Chapter 12.

Taxes

I felt great when I received my first paycheck. I was 16 and making minimum wage, which was $3.35 per hour at the time. I thought that I could multiply my hourly rate by the number of hours I worked to determine how much my paycheck would be. Unfortunately, I didn't realize that Uncle Sam would be getting a pretty hefty chunk of my money. Certain taxes and deductions are subtracted from your paycheck before you receive one penny. These include the following:

Federal Insurance Contributions Act tax (FICA) - This incorporates Social Security and Medicare taxes. Social Security is a program in the United States that provides certain benefits to older Americans, such as a retirement check. Each year that you pay a Social Security tax, the Social Security Administration sends a benefit statement detailing what you paid and what your projected benefits are. Social Security and Medicare make up 6.2% and 1.45% of your gross wages, respectively (employers match those amounts).

Federal Withholding Tax – This is the amount of federal income tax that comes out of your check and is paid to the government. It is based on your filing status (e.g., single, married) and the number of allowances you withhold. For example, if you are married with no children, you can claim two allowances -- one for yourself and one for your spouse. Your employer then uses this information to determine how much tax to deduct from each of your paychecks. If someone else can claim you on their tax return, for example, this would amount to zero allowances.

State/Local Income Tax – Several state and local governments charge income tax to fund operations. However, certain states – Alaska, Florida, Nevada, South Dakota, Texas, Washington, and Wyoming – have no state income taxes.

Things to Remember

1. Consider taking a personality test. They are great, often fun resources that can help you determine what type of career is right for you.

2. Search creatively. There are many ways to look for a new job --- the Internet, newspapers, networking and search firms. Try them all. If you don't see a listing, dare to take a chance. Apply directly to the company you are interested in working for.

3. Be patient and positive. Finding the perfect job takes time. You may receive several rejection letters before landing the right job. But each one just brings you closer to your perfect career.

CHAPTER 8
STARTING A BUSINESS
It takes perseverance, grit and humility to work on your goal and grow from your mistakes.

THE ENTREPRENEUR

E veryone is different; that's what makes all of us so wonderfully unique and helpful to each other. And along with that, everyone has different work styles, attitudes, needs, and values. Some people would rather work for someone else and just not have the responsibilities or even the desire to want to start their own business. It's a certain mind-set; either you really want to do it, or you just don't.

But if you truly have a vision for creating a business of your own, you owe it to yourself to dare to follow your dream. You may stumble with the first venture. But maybe your next one will be the winner, or even the next. But if you stay true to your mission, and if you focus on and know exactly what you want out of it, owning a business can be a rewarding experience with unlimited potential.

Passion

Being an entrepreneur certainly brings many challenges, but having passion for your business makes the hardships worthwhile. When you enjoy what you are doing, you worry less about the money you are making. Your primary focus becomes doing the best job you can.

When I was 12, too young to apply for a traditional part-time job, my older brother and I started a yard maintenance business. Our dad told neighbors about our service and we landed our first clients through his referrals.

I remember he would come with my brother and me to some of the yards we serviced. If we missed even a blade of grass, he would point it out and make sure we cut it. At the time, I thought, "What does it matter if one piece of grass is taller than the rest?" But when I reached adulthood, I understood his message: When you're running a business, the work you do says a great deal about you. Your work is your "personal trademark." If you want to be seen as an entrepreneur with integrity, you must deliver a quality product. That single uncut blade of grass meant the job was not done.

Other neighbors took notice of the good work we did, and we soon garnered more business. We started out with one client, but by the end of the summer we had five, which was all we cared to handle because we wanted time to enjoy our summer break from school.

My dad's lesson stayed with me: Be professional, even if you are working with family and friends. If you say you are going to perform a job at a certain time, keep your word. Give your customers the kind of service you would like to receive. It shows how sincere you are and how much pride you take in your work.

The Business Plan

In the introduction, I gave an acronym for the word PRIDE. The P stands for preparation, and that's what a business plan is – laying the groundwork for how you're going to run your venture. Being successful requires preparation and hard work.

Business plans are often used to help entrepreneurs acquire money from outside investors or secure loans from banks. However, they are also a blueprint for your business. They make you think about what product or service you plan to offer and how you will deliver it to your target market. A well-written business plan will help you grow your business because it includes fundamentals like your mission statement, marketing plan and goals.

Lengths of business plans vary. It may start out as a five-page document, but as your business progresses, it could turn into a fifty-page report. Some simple business concepts can be explained in a few words. But if you're selling a highly technical product, it may take several pages to describe. Write as much as you need to cover the bases.

If you want to use your business plan to raise money from potential investors, write clearly and thoroughly, explaining all of your products or services without too much technical jargon. If not, you may lose potential investors who are unwilling to take on a product they don't understand.

There are many variations of business plans. Here are some of the major elements:

Executive Summary

This section appears first in a business plan, but it should be written after all the other parts have been completed. It gives a short rundown or summary of what the entire proposal is about. This summary is your first – and perhaps only chance – to win the interest of your investors. If it fails to catch their attention, they may not read the rest of your business plan.

Company Overview

Here, you provide a history of your firm. Include information such as the date your firm was founded, plus a discussion of your business strengths and a mission statement that explains why you are starting this venture. Below is a sample mission statement:

Joe's Mobile Detailing was founded to accommodate busy professionals who want to have their vehicles cleaned on a regular basis, but have no time in their busy schedules to wait at a car wash. We go to our clients' homes or businesses to provide a quality exterior and interior cleaning of their vehicles at a good price.

Product Overview

Use this area to share information about the product or service you plan to offer. What are the benefits? Why is it needed now? If you are starting a tutoring business, for example, the benefit to clients could be increased understanding of the subject matter, which could lead to a better grade in a class. In the product overview section, it is also important to explain what makes your product different from the competition. Remember: You want to stand out as the best.

Marketing Plan

The marketing plan is a crucial part of any business plan. It should illustrate your strategy for attracting and attaining new clients. There are many approaches you can use. You can make presentations, pass out fliers, or collect referrals from satisfied customers. The marketing plan should also detail your target market.

Also, maybe your passion isn't something other people are – well, very passionate about! How do you know your idea will sell? This is why you should always conduct some good research to determine whether your product is even needed in today's marketplace. A lot of times, inventors figure they just have to build something wonderful and people will flock to buy it. But again, remember that some (or, in the worst-case scenario) very few people will be interested in your ideas as you are.

So before spending too much time and money, check the marketplace: is there something similar already available? Doing your homework includes thoroughly checking out the competition. Before you even get started, talk to customers of would-be "rival" companies to find out what they like or dislike about a particular product. Also ask what features they would like to see instead.

Market research can also be useful in determining a price for your product. Ask potential customers how much they would be willing to pay for a certain product. If your idea for a product or service is more expensive than the competition, you should have some rationale as to why potential customers would pay more for yours.

Always set goals for growing your firm, and set benchmarks for this: You should never stop setting goals, because you're in business for yourself to make more money as time goes by, right?

Just make sure that your goals are measurable and realistic. For example, a real estate agent may want to add twenty new clients each month. Is that truly attainable? How will he be able to gauge that? By asking other people who are already in the same business. He may find that getting many clients at first may be too ambitious. Sometimes it takes a while to establish a good, solid customer base. If you are consistently falling short on your set goals, you just need to adjust or change them – don't ever take it as a sign that you should give up!

Management

This section of the business plan includes the financial and professional backgrounds on the people who will run your company. If you want to create a web design business, for example, make sure you note how many years you have been a web page designer and if you have taken any related course work or have relevant credentials. If you have any advisers, mentors, teachers, or current or past clients who are helping you with this business plan, mention them, too. A business plan is all about showing where you shine. This is definitely not the time to be modest or shy!

Finding a mentor who has experience with the type of product or service you are offering helps you, and it also looks good. An adviser can serve as a sounding board to let you know the pros and cons of a particular field and offer tips as you go along. And to outside investors, having a mentor shows that although you may not have a lot of experience in a particular area, you have taken the time and care to work with someone professional to guide you as your business grows.

Operational Plan/Milestones

In this section, you will describe in detail how your product or service will be produced. You will also list the supplies and equipment you will need to both start your business and keep it growing. Also, make sure you include at least a good estimate of how many employees you feel you will require to work at your company and what each job function will entail. It's just as important in this section as in any other to dot all the I's and cross all the T's. If you neglect to make sharp, well-thought-out business benchmarks regarding the overall operation of your business, that's going to be a red flag for potential investors. Remember, it takes hard work, dedication, passion, and focus to keep a business running smoothly.

Financial Projections

Financial projections are very important, but put simply, they are an estimate of what you expect your income and expenses to add up to on either a monthly, quarterly, or yearly basis – or all of the above. These numbers matter a great deal to potential investors because they want to invest in businesses in which they are likely to make their money back, plus get a profit. Smart investors know that most new businesses struggle to break even in the early years, but they expect some type of return on their money down the line.

Many businesses fail because of lack of funding. So when you're estimating your cash needs, add some extra padding that will give you more money than you think you need to help pay the bills in the beginning while you build a client base.

Final Details

After you write your business plan, it's always a good idea to have another set of eyes review it to make sure you did not forget any important details. If you can't find someone, see if your city has a Service Corps of Retired Executives (SCORE) chapter. These volunteers are men and women who have spent several years either working for corporations or running their own firms. They've joined SCORE to offer advice to new and existing business owners. They offer free counseling sessions and provide low-cost workshops on topics such as starting a business and writing a business plan.

When you launch a business, there are going to be some areas where you lack expertise – this is not just about you; it's a universal fact. You may have a creative mind and can conceive of innovative products, but you may lack the financial know-how to run a business. Organizations like SCORE and the Entrepreneurs' Organization can provide guidance in areas where you need help.

Family, Friends & Business

When starting a business, it's natural to ask your family and friends for help. But here's the catch: From the very beginning, treat them with the same level of professionalism you would show any investor or customer. Draw up written agreements outlining how you will be using the resources they provide. If you borrow money from them, set up a payment schedule and be sure to pay them back on time. If a friend or relative offers his or her consulting services, be sure to spell out in a contract or letter agreement exactly what service your friend is providing and how much compensation will be paid. Failing to show respect and fairness in your business dealings with loved ones can really put the strain on otherwise close, loving relationships.

NOTES

Things to Remember

1. Choose a business you feel passionate about! If you do, going to work won't ever feel like a chore.

2. Develop a realistic business plan. You may want sales to take off right away, but it may take months or even years before your company starts making a profit.

3. Ask for help. There are going to be areas where you need assistance, so find a mentor to provide advice.

4. Secure funding for your business. Many businesses fail because the owners underestimate how much cash is needed to get it started and keep it going.

CHAPTER 9

EDUCATION NEVER ENDS

*To be a contender in your field
and to reach your earnings potential,
you have to keep learning and growing.*

CONTINUING EDUCATION

I once thought that graduating from college meant I would be free from taking courses for the rest of my life. But I soon found out, quite happily, actually, that education is a never-ending journey.

Many jobs today require more advanced skills than a high school education provides. In the investment industry, there are many certifications required for which you must study in order to "pass." Highly technical jobs require specialized courses or degrees. Careers in health care and computers may require additional schooling because of the continual advances and developments in the field. In many careers, you will also benefit greatly from taking enrichment classes or getting a master's degree or even a doctorate.

Getting an education does not mean you have to go to a four-year college. Community colleges and vocational schools can prepare you for the demands of the workforce as well. The Census Bureau estimates that more than 14 million jobs will be created between 2006 and 2016. They also estimate that fifteen of the thirty fastest-growing occupations will require a bachelor's degree or higher. Some of these occupations include computer systems analysts, financial advisors, and physical therapists.

Studies have shown that higher education leads to more income. According to the Census Bureau, workers without a high school diploma earned an average salary of $22,152 in 2008, compared with those with advanced schooling, who averaged more than $79,000 per year.

Yearly salary calculated by multiplying the median weekly earnings by 52

Salaries for workers 25 and older by education

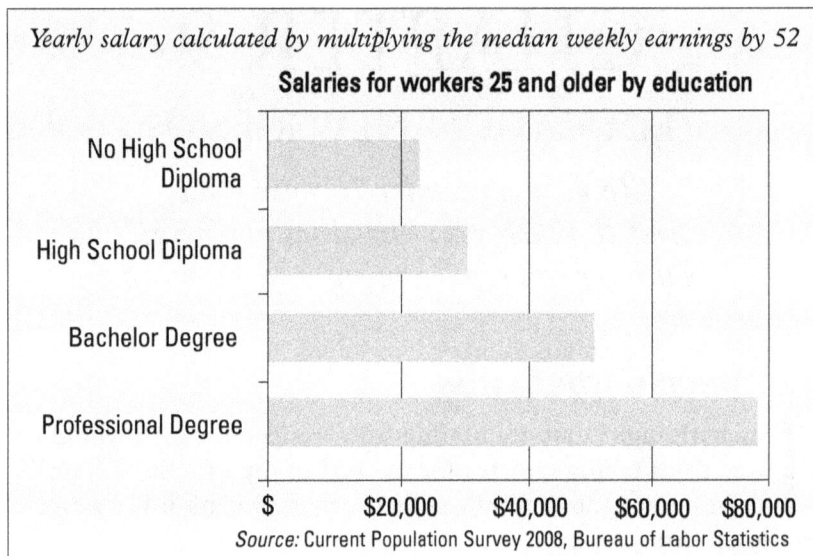

Source: Current Population Survey 2008, Bureau of Labor Statistics

This 2008 survey also revealed that the higher the education level, the lower the rate of unemployment. The average jobless rate in 2008 was 4.5%. The unemployment rate for individuals with less than a high school diploma was about 9%, but it was just 2.8% for those holding a bachelor's degree. The chart below highlights differences in unemployment by education level:

Some say employers prefer more educated employees because they tend to learn faster and can adapt more quickly to change. But it is important to note that a bachelor's degree doesn't mean you'll be exempt from layoffs or that you will automatically make more money than someone with a high school diploma. College graduates get laid off or fired just like everyone else, but having a degree can help you qualify for jobs that are available only to those with a post-secondary education.

Unemployment rate of full-time workers 25 and older by education

No High School Diploma

High School Diploma

Bachelor Degree

Professional Degree

0.00%   2.00%   4.00%   6.00%   8.00%   10.00%

Source: Current Population Survey 2003

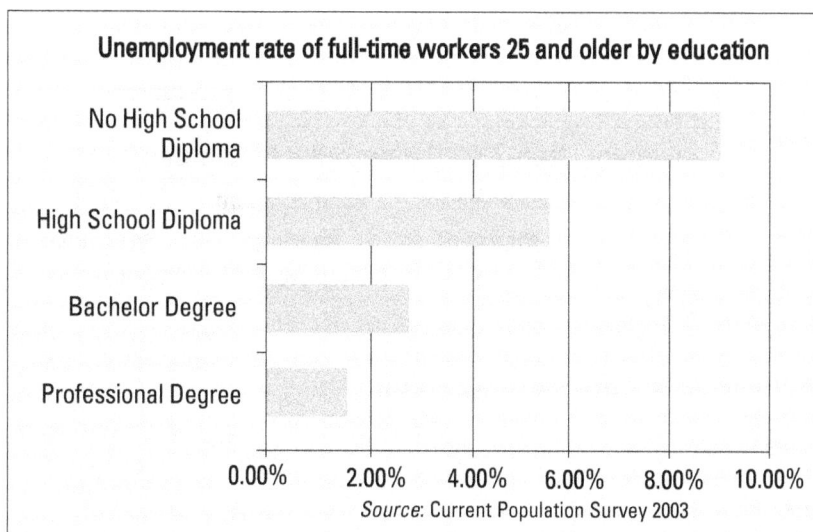

Community Colleges

Community colleges can serve as a good bridge between high school and four-year colleges. They also provide the practical skills necessary to work in certain specialized occupations. If you're unsure about attending college full time, these institutions can be a good option. For one thing, the tuition is cheaper. Associate's degrees and other certifications are awarded, which can upgrade your career. Also, credits you complete at community colleges are often accepted by four-year schools. If you decide to continue your studies and earn a bachelor's degree, you'll already have some of the course work done and can simply transfer those credit hours.

Four-Year Colleges

College tuition costs rise more than 6% every year. That's twice as much as the historical rate of inflation! Just consider this: Inflation is an increase in the prices for goods and services that leads to a decrease in your buying power. According to the College Board, the average cost for a private college's four-year tuition for the 2008-2009 school year is more than $25,000, while public colleges' tuition is almost $6,600 annually.

A college education can be expensive, but consider the benefits such as greater earning potential and the opportunity to apply for jobs that are only available to college graduates.

Average 2008-2009 Undergraduate Charges			
	Tuition & Fees	Room & Board	Total
4 year private	$25,143.00	$8,898.00	$34,041.00
4 year public	$6,585.00	$7,748.00	$14,333.00
Source: College Board			

Education for the Working Adult

Many working adults cannot afford to go back to school full time. They have responsibilities, such as caring for their families, or they may lack the financial resources to pay for a heavy course load. Colleges and trade schools realize that attending classes during the day does not work for everyone. Educators are also realizing that face-to-face interactions aren't the only effective means of teaching. Several schools offer flexible options to help working adults continue their education while working full time. Here are a few:

Online Education

Growing up, I would have never imagined someone could obtain a college degree by taking classes on the Internet. But today, many schools offer legitimate web-based education. Online education programs are convenient for people who don't have the time to physically attend school.

There are two types of programs under Internet education: asynchronous and synchronous:

Synchronous (simultaneous) programs are typically conducted online. Students are required to log in at a specified time for class. Instructors often communicate with students by sending instant messages. The benefit of this type of program is that the instructor is available during the scheduled class time to answer any questions you may have. A drawback is that the class time could interfere with your other activities.

Asynchronous programs allow students to work at their own pace to complete assignments. Instructors place documents on the Internet, which students can then review at their convenience. If you are self-motivated and disciplined, asynchronous education is a great option.

With so many online universities emerging, be sure to do your homework here, as well. Here are some things to consider when choosing an online school:

- Is the school accredited? If so, by whom? Some organizations make up accreditation names to seem credible. Find the proper contact information and call to speak with someone there. Also, check out the Council for Higher Education Accreditation (www.chea.org) to find a list of schools that are accredited.
- Who are the instructors? You can never be too careful. It may sound a little crazy, but check to see if your "instructors" are indeed real people – and that they are qualified. Most Web sites for online schools will have faculty email addresses, so send an email or try to contact them by phone. If the school does not list any names or bios of its staff, be wary of sending money because it could be a scam.
- When was the school founded? Many disreputable schools, such as diploma mills (discussed below), have only existed for a short period of time. The longer the school has been open, the better.
- Does the school offer credit for life experience? Some schools will give credits based on work experience in the military as well as the private sector to help students complete their degrees in a shorter time.

Night & Weekend Programs

If you don't feel comfortable with online classes and would rather sit in a classroom, night and weekend programs may be right for you. I earned my master's degree through night school. I probably could have completed my degree quicker through an online program, but in a classroom setting, I was able to hone skills such as public speaking and working with a team. Just as with the other options, night and weekend programs require lots of discipline. Community and four-year colleges offer degree programs as well as career development classes to help you keep pace with our ever-changing economy. You can pursue a degree or just take one class. Check your local colleges to find out more about their offerings.

Hybrid Programs

Hybrid programs mix attending classes and working on your own to complete course work. You may be required to attend class half of the time and receive the remaining instruction through online or paper-and-pencil assignments. These programs are good for those who would like more interaction with instructors than traditional online classes provide.

Diploma Mills

Have you ever received an ad in your email declaring that you can earn a college degree in a couple of weeks? These companies are known as diploma mills. They award degrees with little or no class work. They are not accredited, but claim to offer authentic college degrees for a flat rate. Below are a couple of emails I received from diploma mills:

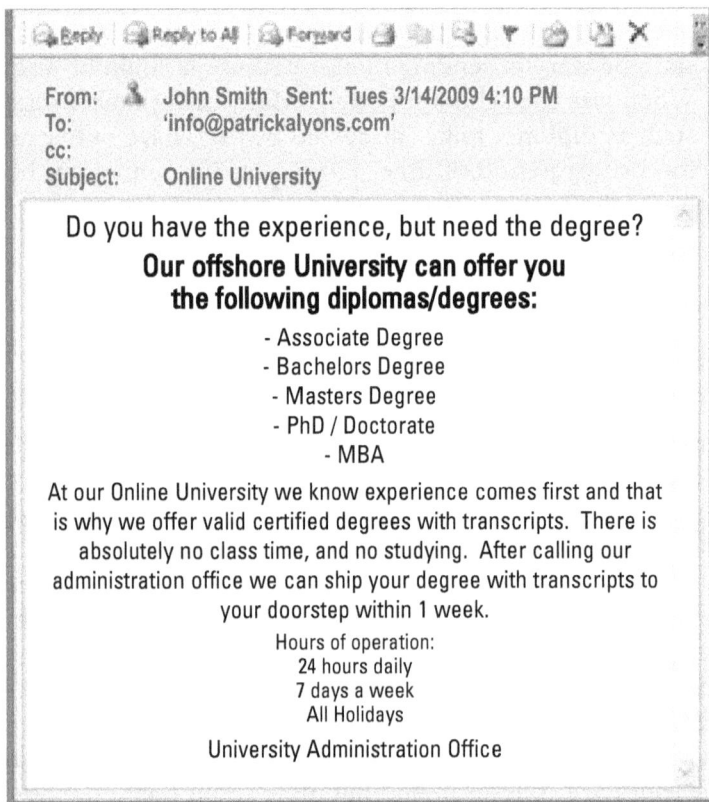

Reply | Reply to All | Forward

From: John Smith   Sent: Tues 3/14/2009 4:10 PM
To: 'info@patrickalyons.com'
cc:
Subject: Online University

Do you have the experience, but need the degree?

Our offshore University can offer you
the following diplomas/degrees:

- Associate Degree
- Bachelors Degree
- Masters Degree
- PhD / Doctorate
- MBA

At our Online University we know experience comes first and that is why we offer valid certified degrees with transcripts. There is absolutely no class time, and no studying. After calling our administration office we can ship your degree with transcripts to your doorstep within 1 week.

Hours of operation:
24 hours daily
7 days a week
All Holidays

University Administration Office

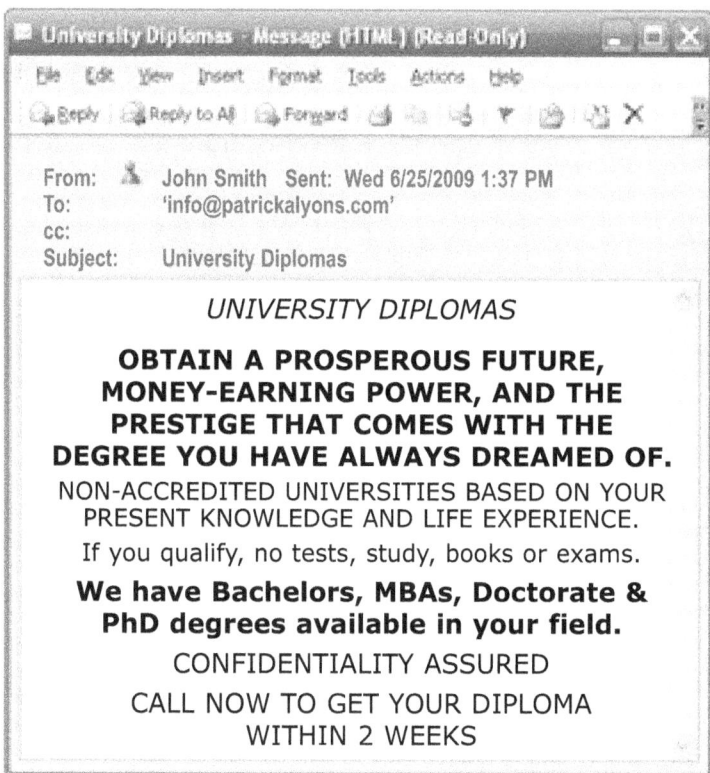

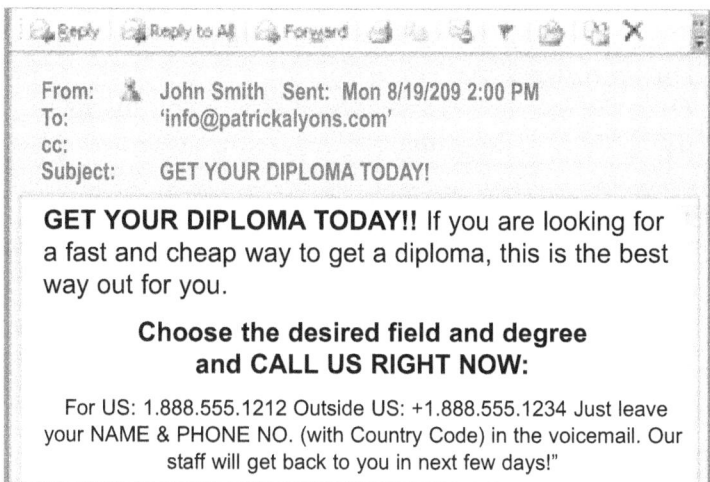

If you are in doubt as to whether a school is a diploma mill, The Council for Higher Education Accreditation recommends asking the following questions. If the answer is "yes" to any of these, it may very well be a fraudulent institution.

- Can degrees be purchased?
- Is there a claim of accreditation when there is no evidence of this status?
- Is there a claim of accreditation from a questionable accrediting organization?
- Does the operation lack state or federal licensure or authority to operate?
- Is little if any attendance required of students, either online or in class?
- Are few assignments required for students to earn credits?
- Is a very short period of time required to earn a degree?
- Are degrees available based solely on experience, or resume review?
- Are there few requirements for graduation?
- Does the operation fail to provide any information about a campus or business location or address and rely only on a post office box?
- Does the operation fail to provide a list of its faculty and their qualifications?
- Does the operation have a name similar to other well-known colleges and universities?
- Does the operation make claims in its publications for which there is no evidence?

Things to Remember

1. Continue your education even if you have no plans to earn a college degree. Certain jobs may require you to take a course, get a certification, or an advanced degree to win promotions.

2. Seriously consider attending college. Studies have shown that over the course of their careers, college graduates average higher salaries than their counterparts with high school diplomas.

3. If you can't attend school full time, consider online schools, night and weekend classes and hybrid programs. Be wary of diploma mills. Many of these organizations will send you a degree for a fee – with no courses required. Be sure to research online schools to make sure they're reputable. And, as a rule of thumb, the longer the school has been around, the less likely it is a diploma mill.

PART 4

CHAPTER 10

RENTING VERSUS BUYING A HOME

Growing older (and just life in general)
brings a lot of major decisions.

One of the two top decisions in most adults' lives is whether to rent or buy a place to live, and to lease or purchase a car. Each choice has its benefits and drawbacks. Your selection process will depend on your situation. In this chapter, we will explore some things to consider as you make up your mind about where to live.

THE BENEFITS OF RENTING

Renting Makes it Easier to Move

When you rent an apartment or house, you sign a lease. This is a legal document that requires you to pay for property you occupy for a specific period of time. But, the good thing about this is that there are ways to end your contract early, if needed.

I bought a house while I was still renting an apartment. I didn't want to pay rent plus a mortgage, so I read over my lease to find out if there was a way I could get out of it. There was. The cost varies to terminate a lease before your agreed-upon date, but it is possible to leave and keep your good credit rating intact. Conversely, if you own a home and decide you want to move, you have to sell your house or rent it out. This process can take months to complete.

Renting Offers Lower Move-in Costs

Rental properties usually charge a security deposit. This amount varies by landlord. One apartment manager asked me for a deposit of just $150. Another required me to put up $400. Some places also ask for the first and last month's rent. This way, if you cause any damage to the apartment, the landlord will use those funds to make repairs so it can be rented again.

I realize that may sound like a lot of money to put up front, just on a rental property. But if you choose to buy a house, you may have to make a down payment, which can cost even more. It can be 3% of the purchase price for a loan with the Federal Housing Administration or at least 5% from other sources. You also need cash for closing costs, which can be several thousands more in out-of-pocket funds.

What Do Home Closing Costs Include?

- **Application Fee** – This is the charge for applying for a loan. Some banks waive this fee. It can be $500 or more.
- **Origination Fee** – This is the amount you will pay to process your loan.
- **Private Mortgage Insurance (PMI)** – If your down payment is less than 20% of the purchase price, the lender may require you to obtain private mortgage insurance. This protects lenders in case you default on your loan.
- **Appraisal Fee** – A licensed appraiser will determine the market value of the house you wish to purchase. The fees vary depending on the type and location of the house.
- **Home Inspection Fee** – This is optional in most cases, but I would highly recommend you hire an inspector to look for defects before completing the purchase of your home. If you are receiving a Federal loan, an inspection may be required. If discrepancies are noted before closing, you can require the seller to correct them or lower the price of the house to account for the repairs. Otherwise, the seller risks you walking away.
- **Credit Report Fee** – This is the charge for the lender, who must run a credit check on you to determine if you qualify for a loan.

- **Attorneys' Fees** – This amount covers the cost of the attorney who handles the legal paperwork.
- **Points** – Lenders charge "points" to reduce the interest rate on loans. One point represents 1% of the value of your loan. For example, one point on a $200,000 loan would be $2,000. Paying one point at closing typically reduces the interest rate on a mortgage by 0.25%. Keep in mind that this is optional. You don't have to pay for points.

Renting Requires Fewer Monthly Costs

Renting a place is far less expensive than buying, at least in the short term. With a rental, you are not required to purchase homeowner's insurance or pay property taxes, but it would be wise to buy renters' insurance to protect yourself from damages that the landlord or apartment manager does not cover. On the other hand, homeowners have to pay for mortgage insurance and sometimes homeowner association dues.

Renting Provides Free or Low-Cost Maintenance

If you rent, the maintenance staff will fix most things that aren't functional in the apartment for free. If you buy, you're on your own. You can either do it yourself or break out the phone book and your checkbook to find someone to solve your problem. Also, if you rent, you may not have to keep up a yard.

THE BENEFITS OF OWNING

Owning Builds Your Net Worth

When you rent, you will never own the apartment or house you are leasing unless it is a rent-to-own plan. When you buy, you can increase your equity (the difference between the current value of your residence and the amount you owe the bank) in two ways. One is by gradually paying down the mortgage principal. The other is through price appreciation. Real estate prices have historically risen by 5% each year, so over time the value of your house will increase. However, there are periods when there is rash of speculative home buying, like we've experienced in Florida and California in recent years where people buy a property only to own it for a few months and attempt to sell, or "flip" it at a profit that can lead to a period of falling home prices when the ranks of buyers drops.

Owning Offers Tax Benefits

Mortgage interest and property taxes are currently deductible on your federal tax return. Points, the amount paid to reduce the interest rate of your loan are also tax-deductible. Another nice benefit is that profits from selling your home are tax-free up to $250,000 for singles and $500,000 for married couples. That's provided you have owned and lived in the property for at least two years.

Owning Stabilizes Costs

If you have a fixed-rate mortgage, your payments will be the same for the life of the loan. The property taxes and insurance may change over time, but the amount paid to your lender will not vary. If you rent, you can usually expect to see the bill increase every year.

Owning Gives You Freedom

When you own a home, you are free to make any changes you want to the interior of the house. Landlords often will not allow you to make cosmetic changes to rental properties because they want to keep costs down and avoid having to repaint walls, re-tile floors, repair carpet, or replace window treatments when you move out.

Buying a house can be an exciting experience, but to make the process go smoothly, we will explore several things to work on before shopping for your home.

Credit Considerations

Whether you are renting or buying, your credit report will be accessed by either the landlord or bank. If you have credit problems, it will be more difficult to buy the place of your dreams. Get a copy of your credit report and ensure that all the information is correct and, if not, get it corrected before applying for a loan. It's also important to note that if your credit score is around 650, you can probably qualify for a prime loan, which is the interest rate offered to customers with the higher credit scores. In addition, if there are no major problems in your credit report and your score is higher than 650, but the lender keeps mentioning the poor credit, then you should look to another source. That said, every borrower should shop around for the right mortgage rate. To find out current interest rates for mortgages, check out sites such as www.bankrate.com or Yahoo! Finance.

Having charge offs and late payments on your credit report will affect the interest rate the bank charges on your mortgage loan. When I got ready to buy my first house, the loan officer looked at my credit report and commented that I had a few charge-offs. She said she could offer me 12% (the rate on a thirty-year mortgage at the time was 7%). That meant I would have to pay an extra $500 per month on the house I wanted because of my bad credit. So, it may make sense to build your credit score if it is below 650 before buying a home rather than buying now and getting stuck with a rate that is not affordable.

My real estate agent told me I might be eligible for a Federal Housing Administration loan (FHA), which is a loan made by a private lender but insured by the federal government. Because I had been current on all of my bills for the twelve months, I did qualify for the loan. I also had to have enough money for the down payment and sufficient income to pay the mortgage.

As a rule, lenders want to make sure the mortgage payment will be no more than 32% of your income before taxes. They also want to ensure that the mortgage and your other debts do not exceed 41% of your pre-tax income. In short, pay your bills on time. When you do, it helps improve your credit scores, which are used to evaluate your credit-worthiness. This makes it easier to buy a house.

Mortgage Brokers

Another option to consider if you have less-than-perfect credit is using a mortgage broker. Brokers specialize in helping consumers with bankruptcies and other bad credit buy homes. It's important to realize if you have a poor credit history, you will pay in the form of high interest rates, fees, or both because you are considered a high-risk customer. However, don't feel that your only choice is an expensive mortgage because you have a couple of late payments on your credit report. You can always choose to rent and strengthen your credit score and apply again in the future.

A mortgage broker has no obligation to get you the best deal, so be sure to ask for a full disclosure of fees. The broker may be paid an amount for his or her services that is in addition to what your lender charges. Also, the broker may receive compensation in the form of a yield spread premium, which is added to your loan at closing. If you feel the costs are too high, negotiate something lower or walk away. Knowing the fees up front empowers you by giving you the information you need ahead of time.

Be sure to get a copy of your credit report before applying for a mortgage to verify the information is correct. The last thing you want is to get rejected for a loan because of incorrect information in your credit file. If you have several late payments noted on your credit report within the last year, you may want to put off buying a house or risk paying a high interest rate that will make that perfect home too expensive.

Types of loans

Fixed rate

A fixed-rate mortgage is one in which the payment does not change for the life of the loan. Lenders offer fifteen- and thirty-year fixed mortgages. A fifteen-year mortgage will allow you to pay off the mortgage faster, but it will require a higher monthly payment than one for thirty years.

Adjustable rate

Adjustable rate mortgages come in several varieties. These loans are paid over a thirty-year period, but the payments are only fixed for a specific time frame, such as one, three, five or seven years. At the time of this printing, the national average rate on a thirty-year fixed mortgage was 5.39%. The rate was 4.58% on a five-year adjustable rate mortgage. These loans carry the risk of rising significantly over a five-year period, which could cause the mortgage at the new rate to be unaffordable when the rate is reset.

Here's how they work: say you receive a loan with an interest rate of 5%. After the introductory period, your interest rate would change based on a benchmark, like the one-year U.S. Treasury bill. Each time the mortgage rate adjusts, it generally goes up no more than 2%, but if your rate went from 5% to 7% on a $100,000 mortgage, your payment would increase by $128 monthly, or 24%, making your mortgage more expensive – and maybe even cost-prohibitive for you. When you received the loan, it was based on your ability to pay a rate of 5% -- not 7%.

There is also the chance that interest rates will go down, which would lower your payment. However, since today's rates are at historically low levels, the odds of lower rates, while possible, is not the most likely scenario. The movement of mortgage interest rates is affected by several factors, such as the growth of the economy, political events and natural disasters, and other unpredictable events.

But if you plan to sell your house before the interest rate on your mortgage changes, then it makes sense to get an adjustable rate mortgage. First, you would benefit from the lower interest rate, and second, by moving before the rate changes, you would avoid the risk of a rise in payment. Also, remember that you can always refinance your adjustable rate loan to a fixed rate at a later date. Just realize that if you go that route you still may not come out ahead because of the fees involved with closing the loan.

Interest-only Loans

Interest-only loans are popular among homebuyers today because you get a low monthly payment, which allows you the opportunity to buy a more expensive house than you could otherwise afford. If you have a $200,000 interest-only mortgage at a 5% APR, the payment would be $833 per month versus $1,074 per month for a loan that requires principal and interest.

It's important to understand that these are still thirty-year mortgages, but just interest is paid for a set time period (usually less than fifteen years). If you pay no principal during that time frame, the amount you owe on the loan would be the same as when you received it. So, a decade later, that $200,000 mortgage you financed would remain $200,000.

When the interest-only period ends, it would be converted to a fully-amortized loan (one that requires principal and interest to be paid). Some of these loans are tied to a fixed rate, but many are adjustable-rate plans where the interest rate is fixed for, say, five years and can fluctuate thereafter.

There are caps that prevent lenders from raising interest rates dramatically when they are reset, but even a 2% increase would cause payments in the example above to rise from $833 per month to $1,167 (40% more). People who use these loans are gambling that either their income will rise so they can afford to pay for the house at the end of the interest-only period, or they anticipate that the value of the home will increase in a short time frame so it can be sold at a profit.

An Interest-Only Loan May Be Suitable For You If:

- You are buying property to live in or rent, but only plan to own it for a short period of time (five years or less).
- You will take the difference between the interest-only payment and a fully-amortized loan payment and use it to lower your principal balance.
- You have the investment savvy to pick stocks or some type of high-return vehicle to grow the money in a short period of time.

Be sure to ask if the loan carries a pre-payment penalty because if you plan to refinance, you may be hit with a hefty charge. If you are selling your home, pre-payment penalties usually don't apply. In light of the current foreclosure crisis, it's important to understand that the value of the home could decline, making the loan worth more than the house. This, in turn, will make it difficult to refinance the loan. In addition, another consideration is your earnings potential. If you are not in an occupation that will guarantee you regular raises in pay to keep pace with interest rate increases, then it's probably best to avoid this type of mortgage.

Pay Extra on Your Mortgage

Regardless of the type of mortgage you choose, it is always a good idea to pay more than your monthly payment. Any extra you send is applied to the principal balance, which means you will pay for your house more quickly. Even if you send an extra $50 per month on a $100,000 thirty-year fixed mortgage with a 5.75% annual percentage rate, you will pay it off five years sooner and will save almost $23,000 in interest. If your payment on the loan is $100 more than the stated mortgage, you would pay it off nearly nine years early, and you would save more than $37,000 in interest charges. That's not chump change!

Some lenders allow for bi-weekly payments (paying half your mortgage payment every two weeks), whereby they make direct debits from your checking account. This method allows you to pay off your loan faster because you are essentially making one extra mortgage payment each year. Using the example above, the loan would be paid off five years early and save you nearly $23,000 in interest. You would have to pay the lender or its administrator a fee for the right to participate in this type of program, so I suggest paying an amount above your monthly payment each month because you can do it on your own without paying an additional charge to a lender.

Subprime Loans

Subprime lenders are firms that lend to borrowers who may not otherwise be able to qualify for loans for conventional loans, such as a thirty-year fixed mortgage. If you have a strong credit score, be careful that you are not steered into these loans because they provide financial incentives to both the broker and the lender, but not the borrower. It's important to do your homework and understand the paperwork before signing anything. That way you can avoid buyers' remorse later, which comes at a steep cost – a yield spread premium and high origination fees.

These loans usually have pre-payment penalties, as well. Pre-payment penalties cause borrowers to incur extra costs if the mortgage is refinanced during the introductory period or before some other pre-determined period spelled out in the mortgage documents. Once you close on the loan, the lender receives his compensation and moves on to the next person.

It's not uncommon to hear from these lenders shortly after you close on the loan to try to get you to refinance the loan, promising a lower payment, or encouraging you to take out a home equity loan to pay off other debts, thereby transferring your equity back to the lender. Don't fall for these tricks. Consider hiring your own attorney to do the closing rather than using the sellers' agent so you can have someone in your corner to explain the paperwork and alert you to any unusual costs added by the lender. By the same token, many real estate agents recommend lenders to clients, so it makes sense to also do some detective work on them to find one you trust instead of someone who may be providing your agent with a financial incentive for steering clients his or her way.

Exploding ARM (also known as 2/28 or 3/27 ARM)

These are adjustable-rate mortgages that start off with an interest rate that may be 1% below the national average for the first two or three years. However, as the name suggests, the rate "explodes" thereafter. The interest rate is typically adjusted every six or twelve months after the introductory period.

Exploding ARMs are appealing to those individuals who have several credit blemishes but are looking for a lower monthly payment than conventional loans. It allows you to qualify for a higher mortgage and thereby buy a bigger house than you may otherwise be able to afford. The problem with these loans is that even if interest rates remain unchanged during the introductory period, the mortgage will still increase because the initial rate was discounted at a lower rate than the current rates when the loan was made.

If you apply for any adjustable-rate mortgages, be sure to read the adjustable-rate rider. It spells out the conditions that will cause your rate to change. For example, let's say you received a 2/28 mortgage for $150,000 at 7.75% two years ago. Today, because of fluctuations in interest rates, your rate would be adjusted to 9.75%. That means the mortgage payment will increase from $1,075 per month to $1,289, up 20%. Keep in mind this does not take into account any increases in real estate taxes or homeowners' insurance.

These loans cause problems for many because they were actually unaffordable from the beginning, but the teaser rate gave the false impression that they were safe.

Payment Option ARM Loans

Option loans have become popular in recent years because they give borrowers choices. Lenders lure borrowers into these loans by saying things like, "It will improve your cash flow because you can choose to pay the low payment." The lender gives a fully indexed rate on this type of loan, like you would receive if you get a thirty-year fixed-rate loan, but the borrower has several payment options to choose from each month.

Traditional payment (includes principal and interest) – This payment is based on a fifteen- or thirty-year term. Choosing this option allows you to pay down the mortgage. On a thirty-year fixed rate loan for $150,000 at 7.5%, the payment would be $1,050 per month.

Interest only – This option will only cover the interest charges, but the principal balance will remain the same. Using the example above, the interest-only payment would be about $940 per month.

Minimum payment – This payment is set as a percentage of the traditional payment, usually anywhere from 50% to 70%. Using the example above, the minimum payment may be 60% of the traditional payment, or $630 ($1050 * .6). If you choose this option, the amount of interest not paid is added to the principal balance. The initial payment may be fixed for a short period of time, like three months, but rise thereafter. This creates a vicious cycle because you will never pay the mortgage down and your monthly payments will continue to rise. This can also make it difficult to refinance because the increase in the value of the loan can outstrip any equity you are building. In addition, you may owe a "balloon" payment, which is a very large payment, at the end of the term if you are just making the minimum payment.

No Doc Loans

If you don't want to share your financial information, then the mortgage industry has the loan for you, but it will cost you some serious change! Some people who don't have steady paychecks because they work on commission, for example, may consider these loans appealing. There are three main types of no doc loans:

Stated income – This loan doesn't require you to submit pay stubs like a typical lender would require, but you will have to submit tax returns for two to three years or profit and loss statements from your business to show how much money you have made. This type of loan will cost more than a conventional loan, but will typically be cheaper than a no-ratio or no-income-verification loan.

No ratio mortgage – Mortgage brokers market also this type of loan to people who don't want to share their financial history with lenders. You will be required to list your assets, such as any checking, savings or retirement accounts, but these loans are very expensive. It's not unusual for these loans to be priced 3% above a conventional loan.

No Income verification – These loans require you to give your name and Social Security number. The factor that determines whether you get this loan or not comes down to your credit score. The higher the score, the less information you will have to provide. If you have a checkered credit past, you may be rejected or asked to provide details about what you do for a living. No-income-verification loans are priced similar to no-ratio mortgages.

Below are a few sample emails I have received encouraging me to refinance into new loans. I know by this time it should go without saying, but please don't fall for these offers!

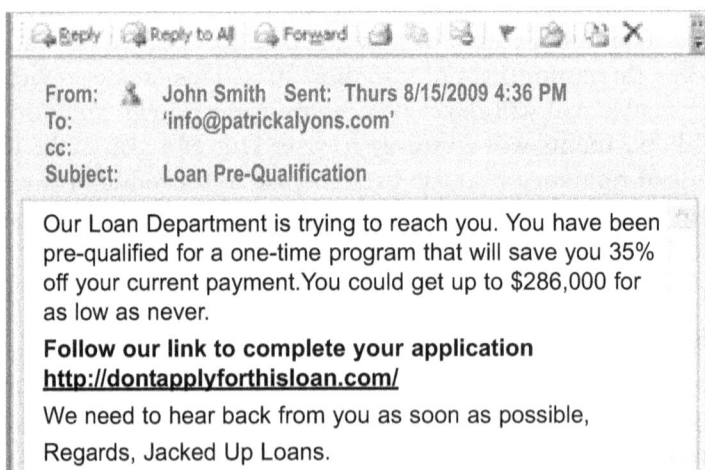

From: John Smith	Sent: Thurs 8/15/2009 4:36 PM
To: 'info@patrickalyons.com'	
cc:	
Subject: Loan Pre-Qualification	

Our Loan Department is trying to reach you. You have been pre-qualified for a one-time program that will save you 35% off your current payment. You could get up to $286,000 for as low as never.

Follow our link to complete your application
http://dontapplyforthisloan.com/

We need to hear back from you as soon as possible,

Regards, Jacked Up Loans.

Reply | Reply to All | Forward

From: John Smith   Sent: Wed 6/25/2009 1:37 PM
To: 'info@patrickalyons.com'
cc:
Subject: Your home has increased in value!

Dear Homeowner,

After a review of your loan history we are happy to inform you that your home has significantly increased in value. This increase enables you to restructure your loan into a newer mortgage with lower monthly payments.

As an additional bonus – Loans that are restructured this month will qualify to skip 2 mortgage payments!

Please call us as soon as possible to take advantage of this offer.

Sincerely, Terrible Mortgage Company

Before you shop for a house:

1)   **Review a copy of your credit report** – Your credit history plays a major factor in getting approved for a mortgage. Look over your report before you apply for a loan to make sure the information is accurate and to avoid any surprises during the application process.

2)   **Get pre-approved** – Once you have your credit in order, go to a bank to get a pre-approval (not to be confused with pre-qualified) letter. The lender will check your credit history and employment information as well as your assets and debts. Then, you will find out the maximum loan value for which you qualify. This can be used as a bargaining chip in negotiations because it shows sellers you can obtain a loan if an offer is made. Some people make offers on houses but cannot qualify for a mortgage.

3)   **Find a reputable real estate agent** – Ask friends and family for recommendations. Another option is to try www.homegain.com. Here, agents compete for your business by presenting proposals on their services. Be sure to interview them to see if they will be able to meet your needs. Find out how long they have been in business. Homegain provides real estate license numbers, so you can check whether any complaints have been filed against the agents you are considering. If you have decided on a particular area of town where you wish to buy property, ask the agent how many homes he or she has sold in the area. Someone knowledgeable of the neighborhood can help you determine a fair market value when you make an offer on a property.

Things to Remember

1. Some people choose to rent because the upfront costs are less than buying a house. Additionally, you have low to no maintenance costs and lower monthly payments.

2. Buying a house has benefits as well, which include a tax break since mortgage interest is tax deductible. Real estate prices have historically risen 5% per year so you increase your net worth if you choose to purchase

3. If possible, avoid subprime loans. If your credit score isn't at a level to qualify for prime interest rates, take the time to repair you credit history to avoid getting in a costly and restrictive loan.

CHAPTER 11

INVESTMENT BASICS

*Here's the goal: Have your money work for you
instead of working for your money.*

W hen I was in college I dreamed of owning a Bentley one
day, but after I graduated with loads of debt, that
thought went out the window. Today, I still think owning
a luxury vehicle is nice, but building wealth is even better. Over
time, the value of a car will decline. If you invest well, however,
your money will grow – and be around for future generations.

A person acquires wealth by buying assets that appreciate over
time, such as real estate, stocks and bonds. Their values may go
down for a short while, but usually rise over the long haul.

We work hard every day to earn a paycheck to provide for our
families and ourselves, but it's even better when the investments
we make generate enough income to cover both our general
expenses and have some left over for savings. This allows us to
work because we want to -- not because it's a necessity.

TYPES OF INVESTMENTS

Stocks

Holding a stock means having ownership in a company. The
more shares you own, the bigger stake you have in the firm.
Every time it makes money, you earn profits as a shareholder.

The flipside is also true. If the company loses money and decreases in value or goes bankrupt, you will also lose money. Stocks are considered risky investments because they can go up or down on any given day. But in the long run, you will benefit from owning stock in a company that is making profits. Your investment could lead to a higher stock price and dividends, which are company earnings that are paid to shareholders.

Stocks are like people. They go through different "phases." A stock's journey begins with an initial public offering (IPO). This is when a company offers stock to the public for the first time. After this phase, stocks usually go through a growth spurt. Companies are usually small- to mid-sized when they go through this period of producing sales and earnings that increase at a brisk pace. Also during this stage, profits are often reinvested into the company to fund future opportunities.

After the growth phase, stocks reach maturity. At this point, the company is usually large and has more consistent and stable profits than growth companies, whose earnings can fluctuate drastically.

These mature companies are sometimes referred to as "blue-chip" stocks. In poker, the blue chips are among the most valuable, and the same holds true for stocks. Blue-chip companies are household names. You've heard them: Wal-Mart, McDonald's, Microsoft. These are companies that have been around for several years and are considered safer investments because they have built a strong reputation in the marketplace. In general, blue-chip companies are more likely to pay dividends than smaller and mid-sized ones.

The last group of stocks is known as "penny stocks." Definitions differ as to what price a company must reach to become a penny stock. Some say that if the price is below $5, that constitutes a penny stock. Others suggest prices below $1 should be considered penny stocks.

These stocks are considered risky, because the companies offering them are small and have little or no operating history. Many firms will send emails to individuals encouraging the purchase of penny stocks. If the stock price is below $1, it is best to avoid buying it because there is a chance it will go out of business, causing you to lose your investment.

More on Penny Stocks

If you're regularly online, you may have received an email claiming to have a "hot" stock tip that will bring big returns in a short period of time. It is common for these emails to feature stocks trading at prices less than $5 per share. Beware of these scams. Do your own research on stocks and never follow a recommendation just because a stockbroker or newsletter is pushing it.

Stock Scam Examples:

Be wary of any emails similar to these:

"Happy New Year........

This one could double by the end of the week. Look for increased volume and huge appreciation. This is only the start of a very aggressive campaign.

Watch this one Rock the Year Year!!!"

"We feel that this is a move for everyday starting Jan 3, 2009

Market Cap: 1.16M
Current Price: $1.87
Short Term: $5.00

As we look for that One Special deal that the public has not come across we Find ABC. We gave it to our Clients one week ago at $1.25 and everyday have watch in amazement as this Company is trading and growing every second. We have no choice but to release this as a Very Special Plat to ALL our clients and say you must watch this first thing Tuesday morning as we see BIG things happening.

WE TELL YOU TO WATCH!!!

STILL NOT TOO LATE!

TRADING ALERT!!!

Timing is everything!!!

Profits of 200-400% EXPECTED TRADING"

"For pennies you can participate in a STOCK that could yield results over and over again just based on the trading patterns if the company is able to effectuate it DKDY'S business model.

WATCH OUT!!!

We could see a GREAT STORY IN THE MAKING."

Analyzing Stocks

There is an old saying that bears repeating here: Invest in what you know. Before buying shares of individual companies, make sure you understand the firm's products and services. I often write a one-page report on the company for my records. It doesn't have to be detailed, but here are some elements it should include:

Company Description – List your overview of the company and its major products or services. You can find this information by visiting the company's Web site or going to Web sites like Yahoo! Finance (finance.yahoo.com); CNN Money (money.cnn.com); and MSN Money (moneycentral.msn.com).

Also, take a look at the company's annual report, a public document that companies present to shareholders on a yearly basis. You can request a hard copy of annual reports or view them online.

Strengths – If you plan to invest your money in a company, it should have some positive factors that make it a compelling buy. Maybe it has more market share than other companies in a particular industry, or maybe it has a niche product that is very important to a certain demographic. I recommend finding at least three company strengths before deciding to invest your money there.

Weaknesses – Although we often have grand plans when we invest in companies, they don't always work out. That's why it's important to understand the firm's weaknesses. Every company has them, so therefore, no stock is perfect.

Remember this: If a stock you invest in doesn't give you the return you had in mind, you can always look back at the company's weaknesses to determine what went wrong. When choosing a stock, make sure the strengths outweigh the weaknesses. Otherwise, it is probably not a wise investment.

BASIC STOCK TEMPLATE

This is an example of a simple one-page report you can put together with just a little time and research:

COMPANY DESCRIPTION

XYZ Corporation is one of the largest consumer electronic retailers in the Southeast. The company offers installation services for home entertainment and computer-related products. XYZ Corporation is headquartered in Jacksonville, Florida, and has 312 stores in seven states. Last year, sales were up 25%.

STRENGTHS

Provides great customer service

XYZ Corporation sends it sales staff through a rigorous on-the-job training program in which it stresses that employees are familiar with and understand the products in their department. Employees don't receive commissions for sales, so there is no conflict of interest with the customer.

Low Prices

Management states that it receives volume discounts by ordering in large quantities. Portions of the savings are passed on to customers.

Internet

XYZ now sells its products over the Internet. This allows the company to reach customers outside the geographic location of its physical stores and could lead to improved sales in the future.

WEAKNESSES

Competition

EFG Stores, the largest consumer electronics retailer in the United States, has been opening stores in the Southeast and plans to build stores near XYZ's in an attempt to win over its customers.

Stock Price Movement

Over the past six months, XYZ's stock price has been up by 25%. Although business appears to be going well, it may make more sense to wait for the stock price to come down before buying.

STOCK MARKET INDICES

If you watch business channels such as Bloomberg, CNBC, or even the network evening news, you'll hear reporters talk about stock market indices like the S&P 500 or NASDAQ. Below are descriptions of some of the more popular ones:

Dow Jones Industrial Average – This is an index of thirty of the largest publicly traded companies in the U.S. Some firms in this index include Coca Cola, General Electric, Home Depot, McDonald's and Wal-Mart.

NASDAQ Composite – This index tracks more than 3,000 stocks listed on the NASDAQ Stock Market. Because technology stocks make up a large percentage of this benchmark, some look at it as a proxy for that sector.

S&P 500 – This index is viewed by many investment professionals as a good representation of the U.S. stock market. It consists of 500 companies that have a broader cross-section of the market than the Dow Jones Industrial Average.

Wilshire 5000 – More than 5,000 stocks are included in this index, making it the broadest measure of stock performance in the U.S.

Bonds

Stocks represent ownership. Bonds represent debt.

A bond is a long-term loan issued by a corporation or government agency in order to raise money. That's where your investment comes in.

When you buy a bond, you're lending money. The issuer pays interest on the loan you've given them, typically twice a year. Usually, bonds are distributed in $1,000 and $5,000 denominations. For example, if you buy a bond with a face value of $1,000 with a 7% interest rate, the corporation or government agency issuing the bond would pay you $70 in interest annually ($1,000 * 7%). And, because interest payments are usually made twice a year, you would receive two checks for $35 each. Upon maturity,(the date the loan must be repaid), you would receive your principal back ($1,000, as in the above example).

U.S. Government Bonds

The U.S. Treasury issues bonds to fund government operations and pay down the national debt. These are backed by the full faith and credit of the U.S. Government; therefore, there is very little chance of default, and these bonds are considered safe investments. But they do have lower interest rates than corporate bonds.

Treasury Inflation Protected Bonds (TIPs)

One of the arguments some investors have against bonds is that they provide minimal returns when you consider inflation. Say the rate of inflation is 3% and your bond is paying 4%. Your real return is only 1% (4% return -3% inflation).

To combat this problem, the U.S. Government created Treasury Inflation Protected Bonds, also known as TIPs. Similar to traditional bonds, holders of TIPs receive interest payments twice a year. However, unlike traditional bonds, where your principal is set for the term, TIPs are adjusted based on the Consumer Price Index (CPI).

The CPI is the most commonly used measure of inflation in the United States. If the economy is in an inflationary environment, the principal will be increased based on the increase of the CPI. If the CPI is declining (deflationary), the principal balance of your bond will decline. At maturity, you will receive either your original principal balance or adjusted balance, whichever is greater.

Corporate Bonds

Companies issue bonds for a number of reasons: to buy new equipment, build a new facility or finance current operations, for example. Corporate bonds typically pay higher interest than comparable government bonds, but they carry additional risk. If a company goes bankrupt, it may not be able to make interest payments. Although bondholders would recover their money before stockholders in such an event, there is a chance that you would only receive a fraction of your initial investment or nothing at all. Also, the interest you receive on corporate bonds is taxed.

Municipal Bonds

Municipal bonds are issued by state and local governments to pay for projects such as schools and road repairs. The interest received on these loans is usually exempt from state and local taxes, provided you reside in the state where you bought the bond. The interest rate is lower than a corporate bond with the same maturity, because the interest on a municipal bond is tax-free.

For example, if you have a corporate bond that pays 6% and a municipal bond that pays 5%, to determine which bond is better, you need to add back the tax to the municipal bond.

Here's a simple formula to "do the math": $R/(1 - t)$, where R is the interest rate on the municipal bond and t is the tax rate. Assuming you are in the 28% tax bracket and are receiving 5% interest, the formula would look like this: $0.05(1-.28)$, which equals 6.94%. This is clearly higher than the 6% from the corporate bond, so in this case, the municipal bond is a more attractive investment opportunity when you adjust for taxes.

Bond Quality Ratings

Just as consumers have credit scores, bond issuers receive ratings. The two main bond rating agencies are Standard & Poor's and Moody's. They grade companies on their abilities to make interest payments and repay the bonds in full at maturity.

For Standard & Poor's, the highest rating an issuer can achieve is AAA, while the lowest is CC.

Any bond rated below BBB is considered a "junk" bond. Just as individuals with bad credit have to pay higher interest rates for loans, companies with poor credit ratings have to pay investors a high interest rate for taking on the risk. Junk bonds offer better interest rates than higher-quality bonds, but there is a good chance the bond issuer may not be able to pay the interest because it does not have enough cash.

As an example, below is a table with Standard & Poor's ratings:

Standard & Poors Ratings	
Rating	**Description**
AAA	Highest rating. Extremely Strong
AA	Very Strong
A	Strong
BBB	Good
BB	Marginal
B	Weak
CCC	Very Weak
CC	Extremely Weak

NOTES

International Investing

It's important to remember although the U.S. market is the largest, more than 50% of the world's stock market value is outside of America. By just focusing on what's offered at home, you may miss out on opportunities to participate in growth around the globe. Emerging markets such as India, China, and Brazil are currently growing more rapidly than the U.S. market.

Investing internationally can enhance returns by giving your portfolio exposure to faster-growing economies and lower risk because the fluctuations differ from our markets. Just because a certain category of U.S. stocks are going down, for instance, does not mean stocks in other countries are. Although international exposure can increase returns, always remember -- it does carry risk.

If you have a mutual fund prospectus and read the fine print, you will see this statement: "Past performance is no indicator of future performance." Just because a particular market enjoys strong returns one year is not a guarantee that it will continue.

There is also currency risk. If the U.S. dollar goes up in value, it will lower the value of any foreign investments you own. This is because when you sell the securities, you will have to convert them back into U.S. dollars, which will be worth less because of the dollar's strength.

One final risk to consider is political unrest. Countries experiencing military coups or other types of turmoil will most often negatively influence the stock and bond markets in that particular region.

To make things flow more smoothly when engaging in international investing, one of the easiest ways to invest is to buy an international mutual fund. Portfolio managers have knowledge of the region and may actually live there. They can use their skill in constructing a portfolio of stocks that reduces risk for you.

Real Estate

Particularly in today's economic climate, it's a very good idea to consider adding real estate investments to your retirement portfolio. There are a number of ways to do this, but one of the easiest is by using real estate investment trusts (REITs). Unlike real estate transactions, in which you buy or sell property using agents, which can cost several thousands of dollars, REIT offers exposure to a portfolio of real estate investments by buying just one share from your stockbroker and paying a minimal commission.

The National Association of Real Estate Investment Trusts Index averaged an annual return of 6.83% from 1998 to 2008, easily outpacing the performance of stocks (-13.70% for the S&P 500).

A REIT is a company that invests in real estate directly or buys mortgages. It may invest in shopping malls, hotels, apartments or office buildings. These trusts must pay out at least 90% of earnings in the form of dividends, so they typically offer higher dividends than most stocks and bonds.

You also receive a tax benefit with your investment. Corporations must pay taxes on their earnings, and dividends to those who own stock are taxed, so they are subject to double taxation. However, REITs do not pay corporate income tax so you are taxed just once, on the dividends you receive.

Another benefit is that you can buy REITs from your broker, just like you would with any stock or mutual fund, which is faster and less expensive than using a real estate agent.

The final advantage of REITs is liquidity. Because they are listed on the major stock exchanges, all you have to do is place a trade with your stockbroker, and you can sell those stocks that day. This is of course in contrast to selling a piece of property, which may take months or even years because it takes time to find a willing buyer.

Commodities

Commodities are products we consume such as coffee, orange juice, meat products (hogs, beef, chicken); or grains (wheat and corn).

Commodities are also items we use, such as precious metal (gold, silver, platinum); and energy (crude oil, natural gas, unleaded gas). During the past few years, we have felt the effects of rising gas prices because of various factors, such as the war with Iraq and hurricanes that damaged oil refineries in the Gulf of Mexico.

In cold weather, we consume more energy, which raises the price of heating oil and natural gas, requiring us to pay more to heat our homes. A few years ago, there was a "Mad Cow" scare, which caused the price of cattle to go up, making it more expensive to buy beef products.

I know you may not often think of commodities as an area in which to invest for retirement, but here's the key: You can actually profit from price increases in the products you use every day.

Most assets, such as stocks and bonds, are hurt by inflation. However, though rising commodity prices are an indication of inflation, you can buy things like gold or oil stocks to actually profit from inflation.

If there is an unexpected increase in inflation, for instance, stock and bond market averages may decline, but commodities may rise because higher prices mean increased demand for the raw materials used in the goods we consume. This protects investors against inflation.

An easy way to invest in commodities is to buy a mutual fund or exchange traded fund, which invests only in commodities. We'll cover that later in this chapter.

Diversified Investment Choices

For investors who lack the time or desire to choose their own stocks and bonds, mutual funds and exchange traded funds offer a broad exposure to investment choices – and with low minimum investments.

Mutual Funds

Mutual funds are financial instruments that allow investors to pool their money together. Portfolio managers are responsible for deciding which securities are purchased and sold.

The most common types of mutual funds are stocks, bonds and balanced funds. Balanced funds are a combination of stocks and bonds. Stock funds can be further divided into other classifications, based on the types of securities purchased. Some of these include:

Market Value – Some mutual funds only buy stocks of companies within a specific market value range. You will have mutual funds that may only invest in small, mid-sized, or large companies.

Geographic Location – These are mutual funds that invest only in U.S.-based companies or other specific regions of the world.

Style – Yes, even stocks have "style!" You may hear the terms "growth fund" or "value fund" from time to time. A growth fund invests in stocks that are expected to increase faster than the average company.

Now, with the prospect of quick growth comes more risk. But remember, the younger you are, the more risks you can afford to take. A 22-year-old, for example, may want to consider having a greater allocation of growth stocks in his or her portfolio than a 65-year-old retiree. The younger person has several years to make up for any stock market losses, whereas the older person is more likely to depend on more conservative, "here-and-now" investments.

Value stocks, on the other hand, produce slower and more stable earnings. They are less volatile and are perceived to be less risky than growth stocks. Value funds also typically have a higher dividend yield, making them an attractive investment choice for those looking for income producing stocks.

Index – There are several types of indices that mutual funds can track. There are broad ones, such as the Wilshire 5000 Index, or narrow ones, which follow a specific sector of stocks, like computer-related companies.

For investors who have little desire in outpacing the returns on the major stock market averages and want to pay lower fees, index funds make a lot of sense. Fees on index funds average 0.20% annually versus the average mutual fund, with fees exceeding 1%.

The major benefit of a mutual fund is that you can own a diversified portfolio of securities with a smaller investment than it would cost to purchase several stocks on your own. Some mutual fund "families" will allow you to start with as little as a $500 initial investment.

MUTUAL FUND FEES

Front end load – This fee is used to pay commissions to a salesperson. It is charged during the first year of owning a mutual fund and can range from 3% to 8.5%.

Back end load – The opposite of a front-end load, this means you pay your sales charge when you sell instead of when you buy. This fee averages 3% and is deducted when you sell your mutual fund shares. If you own the mutual fund for a number of years, usually seven, you won't be charged a back-end load.

Redemption fees – These are charged by some mutual funds to discourage short-term trading. Some investors want to constantly switch between mutual funds, so some firms use redemption fees to discourage this kind of "jumping around." If fund shares are sold within a short period of time (usually one year), the investor may be subject to fees as high as 2%.

12b-1 fees – This covers the cost of advertising and promotions for the fund. By law, this fee cannot be more than 0.75% of your investment.

Management fees – Portfolio managers and their support staff must be paid for their work. As such, they receive the management fee, which averages 0.50% of your investment.

Expense ratio – When you add up all of a mutual fund's costs mentioned above, you end up with an expense ratio.

Exchange Traded Funds (ETFs)

Exchange traded funds are baskets of stocks that mirror the portfolio of a particular stock or bond index. It may be a broad one like the Russell 3000, or a narrower one, such as the Dow Jones Energy Sector.

There are currently more than 800 ETFs offered in the United States. I am a big fan of ETFs because they are an easy way to carry out an asset allocation strategy, which will be discussed in Chapter 12. Here are a few of the benefits of ETFs versus mutual funds:

Transparency – You can go to www.amex.com each day to find out which securities are held in a particular ETF. Mutual funds don't disclose holdings to investors on a daily basis.

Flexibility – ETFs are priced continuously throughout the day, allowing you to buy or sell at specific prices, like you would for stocks. Mutual funds are priced only once daily, at the end of the day.

Diversification – You get instant diversification by buying just one share of an ETF. For example, one share of the S&P 500 ETF gives you exposure to the 500 stocks in that index.

Some mutual fund companies require minimum deposits of $5,000 or more to open an account. With ETFs, you can buy as many or as few shares as you wish, but you will have to pay a commission to your stockbroker each time you purchase or sell. They're a great way to start investing if you don't have a lot of money.

For more information check on exchange traded funds, check out www.amex.com.

Annuities

Purchasing annuities is another way to plan for retirement. Since many companies are getting rid of pension plans that pay retirees a fixed amount for life and are replacing them with defined contribution plans such as 401(k) and 403(b) plans that leave it up to the employee to make investment decisions, annuities can be helpful by providing a stable source of income. These investment products guarantee a monthly payment which can continue for the rest of your life. This is great if you feel you will outlive your savings or have chronic medical problems that require monthly prescriptions and other costs on an ongoing basis.

However, all annuities are not transferable, so if you die, your heirs may not get the money. You do get a tax break for funds invested in annuities. You only pay taxes once you start receiving payments. If you are looking at this type of product for tax reasons, consider maxing out on low-cost tax-deferred vehicles like IRAs and 401(k) plans first before using annuities, which usually come with high sales charges.

Things to Remember

1. Owning a share of stock represents ownership in a company. If you decide to buy an individual stock on your own, do your homework and make sure you understand what you're getting.

2. When corporations or government agencies want to borrow money, they issue bonds. Most bonds pay interest on a semi-annual basis. U.S. Treasuries are among the safest bonds to invest in because they are backed by the full faith and credit of the federal government, whereas corporate bonds are more risky because a corporation may go bankrupt and not be able to repay its bondholders.

3. With mutual funds and exchange traded funds, you have the opportunity to build a diversified portfolio for much less than you would pay by purchasing individual stocks and bonds on your own.

4. Real estate investment trusts are like mutual funds because they are a collection of investments, but they invest solely in real estate. This is a low-cost way of buying and selling real estate because transactions can be completed by placing a trade with your stockbroker as opposed to going through a real estate agent, which can take months to complete.

5. Commodities are raw materials used to produce a lot of products we find in our everyday life such as coffee, orange juice or gasoline. Investing in these assets is a good way to protect yourself against the effects of inflation. Increased demand for goods will lead to higher commodity prices, which in turn leads to higher prices for the products we use.

CHAPTER 12

RETIREMENT PLANNING

It is important to take retirement planning very seriously.

According to the National Health Center for Health Statistics, in 2006 the average life expectancy for Americans was 78. Some individuals are living long enough to spend a significant portion of their lives in retirement, and if you are like me, you don't want to work until you kick the bucket, so start saving while you are young so that when you retire, you can enjoy it. If you start planning for retirement early in your career, you are not guaranteed a successful financial retirement, but it certainly puts time on your side, which can increase your odds of being successful in achieving your financial goals.

BROKERAGE ACCOUNTS

Typically, when you buy or sell publicly traded stocks or bonds, you do so through a brokerage firm. Full-service brokers provide extra service such as research that can be used in picking investments. In addition, they may offer products and services such as insurance and estate planning. Discount brokers, on the other hand, offer lower commissions to conduct investment transactions, but don't offer all the other services. It's a no-frills way of investing.

I have seen discount brokerage commissions as low as $5 per trade. It's not uncommon to find a full-service broker that starts commissions at $50 per trade. If you do your own research on the investments you buy, then a discount broker is the way to go because you will save a lot of money.

RETIREMENT ACCOUNTS

IRAs

IRAs, or Individual Retirement Accounts, allow you to save for retirement and receive some tax benefit at the same time. There are two basic types of IRAs: Roth and Traditional. An IRA is a savings option for employees of companies that don't offer any other type of retirement vehicle such as 401(k)s or pensions. In addition, individuals who want to save above and beyond their contributions to company-sponsored plans can choose to open an IRA.

Roth IRA

Earnings grow tax-free in a Roth IRA; however, contributions are made with after-tax dollars. In 2009, the income limit was $105,000 for singles and $166,000 for married couples. If your income exceeds those limits, you can contribute to a non-deductible IRA, but not a Roth IRA. Withdrawals made after you reach age 59 ½ are tax-free. In addition, if the account has been open for at least five years, you can withdraw contributions without a penalty.

Traditional

Traditional IRAs will give you a tax break today (provided your income doesn't exceed income limits ($65,000 for singles and $109,000 for couples, in 2009), but you will have to pay taxes on withdrawals at your current tax rate. You may be in the 33% tax bracket while you are working full time; however, in retirement you could potentially fall to the 15% tax bracket (assuming your income drops). So although there will be a tax burden, it won't be as much as if you were working full time. Because these accounts were designed for retirement purposes,

there are penalties if you make withdrawals before age 59 ½.
There are certain exceptions for situations such as buying your
first home, paying medical expenses, or death.

IRA Summary

One thing to consider when you set up an IRA is that
traditional IRAs can be converted to Roth IRAs. However, a
Roth IRA cannot be switched back to a traditional IRA, so make
sure you think carefully before opening this type of account. Also,
if your income exceeds the annual limit for traditional IRA, then
a Roth IRA makes sense because at least your earnings grow tax-
free even though your contributions are not tax deductible.

Deciding which type of IRA to open basically comes down to
whether you want to pay more in taxes now or in the future –
there's just no getting around taxes in life, right? But for example,
while contributions to traditional IRAs are tax deductible today,
withdrawals are taxed. Roth IRA deposits are not tax free, but
certain withdrawals made after the account has been set up don't
incur taxes. Regardless of whether you choose a Roth or
Traditional IRA, you have more flexibility in picking your
investments. The 401(k) plans typically offer a limited number of
mutual funds to choose from, whereas you can choose to buy as
many individual stocks with an IRA as you choose.

Traditional versus Roth IRAs

	Traditional	Roth
Tax free withdrawals	No	Yes
Tax Deductible Contributions	Yes*	No
Tax Deferred Growth	Yes	No
* Subject to income limits		

Defined Benefit/Pension Plans

A pension plan will pay you a fixed amount each month after
you retire. These plans are sometimes referred to as defined

benefit programs because you know in advance what you will be receiving. Organizations that offer these plans have different ways of calculating how much you will be paid. Some may base it on the number of years of service, while others take a percentage of your salary. Employees do not have to make contributions to these plans because employers assume the responsibility and also make investment choices on their behalf.

It's great if you can find a company that offers a pension, but they are becoming a thing of the past as more companies and government organizations are now shifting the burden to employees by switching to 401(k) plans. Some companies are making the change because people are living longer today than they did in the past. Firms with pension plans make assumptions on the returns they need from investments in order to meet their obligations and pay benefits to retirees. From 2000 to 2003, U.S. stock market returns were negative, which means it cost companies more to maintain these plans because their stock market projections were too optimistic.

401(k)/403(b)

The 401(k) and 403(b) plans are personal retirement plans for employees. Most large companies and many small companies offer employees 401(k) plans. The 403(b) programs are offered to employees at educational institutions as well as some non-profit organizations. Both plans are similar, so the discussion that follows will focus on 401(k) programs.

With these plans, companies may match your contributions up to a certain percentage, but ultimately it is up to you to make investment choices. Just as companies with defined benefit plans make assumptions on various factors affecting pensions, you will have to figure out how much you will need in retirement.

There are a number of calculators on the Internet that can assist you, such as Bank Rate (http://www.bankrate.com/brm/calc/401k.asp) or www.banksite.com (http://www.banksite.com/calc/annuity2). These calculators ask how much of a return you expect each year, and I suggest using a number between 7% to 10%. You may earn more from your investments, but this gives you a reasonable estimate to start with. Once you determine the amount needed to achieve your goal, you can develop a savings plan.

You should contribute as much as possible to your 401(k) because in 2009, your contributions are tax deductible up to $16,500. In addition, by participating in these plans you have the opportunity to get "free money" if your employer matches your deposits. Your contributions vest immediately, which means that if you decide to leave the company, you will own 100% of your contributions and earnings. Company contributions may vest over a period of years.

VESTING

The three types of vesting are immediate, cliff and graduated.

Immediate – In this scenario, all your contributions vest right away. Some companies also have retirement plans in which its contributions become yours as soon as you become a participant in the plan.

Graded Vesting (Graduated) – With this type of plan, you earn a portion of your employer's contributions each year. In the case of five-year vesting, you will own 20% of your employer's contributions in your first year. In the second year, it jumps to 40% and continues until the fifth year, at which time you would own all contributions made by your company.

Cliff vesting – With cliff vesting, you own all contributions after you have been on the job for a certain number of years. For example, if the company uses a period of three years, you would own all contributions made by your company after year three. If you leave during your second year, you would receive all of your deposits, but none of employer's.

If your company offers a 401(k) plan, I strongly encourage you to participate. Even if you can only contribute 1% of your salary, it can make a difference over time. The charts below show the value of starting your investment plan early. The first chart assumes a salary of $24,000 with a 3% contribution from you, and a 3% matching contribution from your employer. I also assumed a 9% annual return on your investments. If you have 40 years until retirement, your balance would accumulate to more than $500,000 by investing just $60 per month.

Employer Matching 3% Contribution

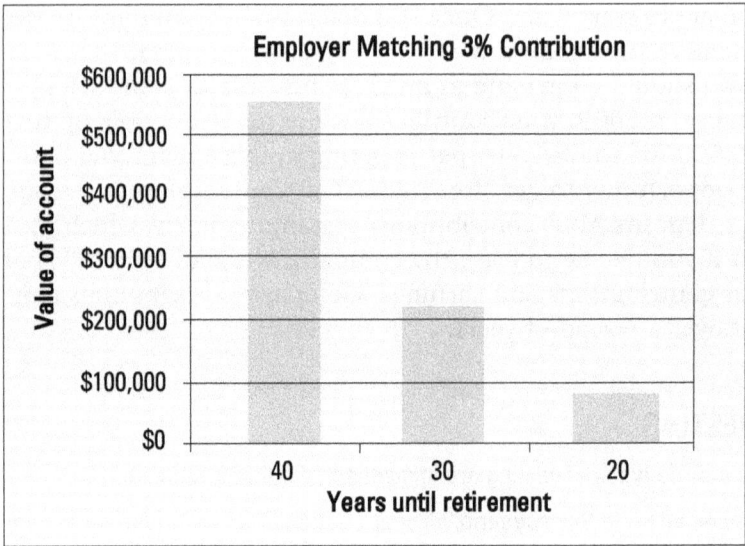

The chart below assumes a $24,000 salary with the employer matching a 5% contribution from the employee. As you can see, if you have 40 years until retirement, your account value will grow to over $900,000 versus $134,000 for the person who opens an account just twenty years before retirement.

Employer Matching 5% Contribution

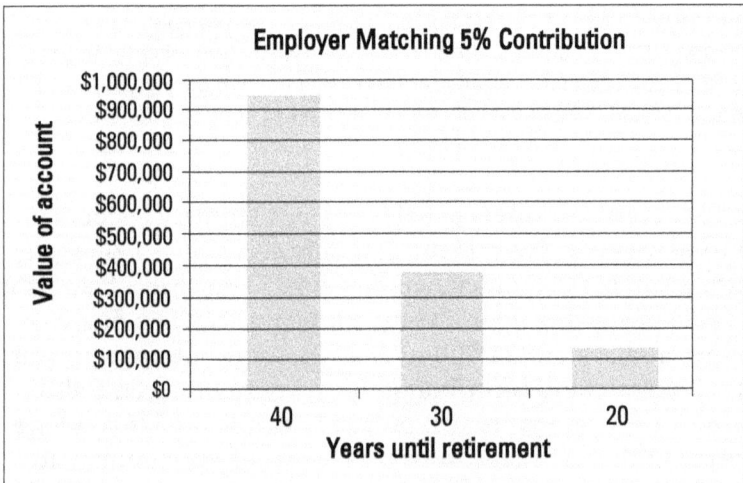

These scenarios don't take into account the fact that you may receive raises or increase your contributions over time, so the message is to start early. It also doesn't take very much money, either. The 3% example only requires $60 per month from you, while you need to contribute $100 monthly if you choose 5% of your salary. And making these types of savings decisions should not sacrifice one's lifestyle dramatically.

Withdrawals

There is a 10% penalty for withdrawals made before you reach age 59 ½. However, withdrawals are allowed without penalty for the following reasons:

- Buying a home
- Medical expenses for yourself or dependents
- Certain post-secondary educational expenses
- To prevent eviction or foreclosure from your primary home.

You can also take out loans from your 401(k) account. Some suggest this is a good way to get a loan for emergencies. I would not recommend it unless it is a last resort. Loans must be repaid with interest, which means you will essentially be paying yourself back with interest. The downside is that if you leave the company before you repay the loan, the balance is due immediately. If you don't have the funds to repay at that time, the loan is treated as a withdrawal, which is subject to tax penalties.

Rollovers

Today many people change jobs more frequently than they did several years ago. This has created a problem for many of us, because it leaves us wondering what to do with money left in our 401(k) accounts. In some cases, people withdraw the money and spend it. If you absolutely need the money right away, you need it, but this will be taxed because the withdrawal is considered income and will have to be reported on your tax return.

It is wiser to transfer the money to the retirement plan at your new employer or roll it over into an IRA. Using an IRA gives you more flexible investment options. Typically, 401(k) plans limit your choices. If you go this route and don't have the time to monitor your investments, consider hiring a financial advisor to do it for you.

PUTTING IT ALL TOGETHER

You want to create a diversified portfolio consisting of stocks, bonds, commodities and real estate. Traditionally, stocks and bonds are the easiest in which to invest, but with the introduction of exchange traded funds and new mutual funds, real estate and commodities are now available to the average investor. The benefit of having commodity and real estate exposure is that these asset classes do not perform entirely like stocks or bonds and can thus lower your overall risk, while potentially boosting returns. As far as stocks are related, make sure you have exposure in U.S. and international stocks. There is literally a world of opportunity outside the United States, and the performance of international stocks, like commodities and real estate, is not connected to U.S. stock price movements.

ASSET ALLOCATION

What is asset allocation?

Asset allocation is the process of dividing your investment funds between the major asset classes (stocks, bonds, real estate, commodities, etc.) to get the highest return and manage risk. Some may refer to asset allocation as not "putting all of your eggs in one basket." The younger you are, the more risk you can afford to take. So, a 21-year-old should own more risky investments like growth and international stocks than someone closer to retirement age.

Why is This Important?

Studies have shown that asset allocation accounts for a majority of investment returns. Therefore, picking the right stock isn't as important as having broad exposure to several asset classes (e.g., U.S. stocks, international stocks, bonds, real estate and commodities). Since the performance of each group isn't dependent on the other, it reduces risk. So if stocks are going down in the face of weak economic news, bond, commodity, and real estate prices may rise because they are driven by totally different factors.

The good thing about asset allocation is that you don't have to be right on one particular asset class because you have exposure to other groups that may be going up while others are declining. Unfortunately, many investors focus only on the stock market and miss out on opportunities in the other investment groups. You may own a stock mutual fund and decide to sell because stocks are going down and leave your proceeds in cash until you feel comfortable owning stocks again. Meanwhile, commodity prices or bonds are rising, but you would have missed out on that opportunity because your money was sitting in cash.

Don't try to time the market. If you have time on your side and a disciplined strategy, you will make money in the long run, so let your money work for you by investing it in vehicles that will make you money. I am reminded of a quote by John Shedd: "A ship is safe in harbor, but that's not what ships are made for." Parking money in checking and money market accounts will not generate much of an investment return. You have to be willing to take some risks if you want to create a nest egg for retirement.

How You Can Implement Asset Allocation

If you search the Internet, you can find tons of advice on what percentage of stocks and bonds to own. One popular school of thought is to have 60% of your portfolio in stocks and 40% in bonds. The problem with this strategy is that you miss out on real estate and commodities. Also, it does not change over time. You should have a dynamic plan that changes based on your age or risk tolerance.

As a first step in determining how to allocate your money, consider your age. This number is the amount you should have invested in bonds. If you are 20, then you should designate 20% of your portfolio to bonds. The bond portion will increase as you get older and want a more stable source of income. Someone who is 75 is older and is more concerned about receiving the interest payment checks from bonds than getting growth out of stocks.

TIPs are a great idea for the bond portion of your portfolio because they protect you in the event of inflation. Although they can decline if we are in a deflationary environment (falling prices), you will never receive less than you initially invested. Next, designate from 10% to 15% of your portfolio to real estate and commodities. These asset classes help reduce risk because their movements aren't tied to stock or bond price movements. The remaining amount should be invested in stocks.

While you are young and have several years until retirement, it's a good idea to have the majority of the stock portion invested in small- and mid-sized growth companies because you have time on your side and can make up any losses that come with owning these riskier investments. Also, have at least 10% of your stock exposure earmarked for international stocks. As I mentioned earlier, several stock markets around the world are growing faster than the U.S. market, and owning an international mutual fund can increase returns of your overall portfolio. Once you determine your asset allocation levels, stick with your plan. Portfolios should be reviewed at least quarterly. Try not to do too much buying and selling in a short period of time because it could generate short-term capital gains, which eat away your profits because they are taxed at a higher rate. Don't be afraid to hire a professional to help set up your strategy because your financial future depends on the decisions you make today.

BENCHMARKING

According to the American Heritage Dictionary, a benchmark is a standard by which something is measured. Although I discourage short-term trading, it is still important to measure performance of your mutual funds against some yardstick. Some of the more popular stock market indices are the Dow Jones Industrial Average and the Standard & Poor's 500. However, there are benchmarks for mutual funds, too. Below are a few to consider:

Stock Mutual Funds – Lipper Multi Cap Core Funds Index, Russell 3000 (http://www.russell.com)

Bond Mutual Funds – Lipper General Bond Funds Index, Barclays Government/Credit Index (http://group.barclays.com)

Real Estate Investment Trusts – Lipper Real Estate Funds Index, National Association of Real Estate Investment Trust Composite REIT Index (http://www.reit.com)

Commodities – Lipper Natural Resources Funds Index, Reuters/Jefferies CRB Index (http://www.jefferies.com/RJCRB/)

International Stocks – Lipper International Funds Index, Lipper Mutual Fund indices at http://www.lipperweb.com.

If you find a fund has underperformed its benchmark for 3 consecutive quarters you may want to consider making a switch unless you are comfortable that performance will turn around.

NOTES

Things to Remember

1. IRAs are personal retirement savings accounts that you can set up on your own. They are independent of any plan your employer may offer.

2. The two main types of IRAs are Roth and Traditional. Contributions to Roth IRAs are not tax deductible, but your earnings grow on a tax-free basis. Traditional IRAs, on the other hand, allow for contributions to be tax deductible, provided your income has not exceeded the level set by the IRS.

3. If your company has a retirement savings plan such as a 401(k), participate if you are eligible. It is a way of saving for the future and getting "free money" if your employer matches your contribution.

4. Asset Allocation is the process of spreading your investment funds among different asset classes (e.g., stocks, bonds, real estate, commodities) to reduce risk and increase returns.

CHAPTER 13

PLANNING FOR THE UNEXPECTED

*Most of us would rather not think about estate
planning until we reach retirement age.*

You know how it goes – we graduate from school, get married, have kids and enjoy life. Who has time to think about boring stuff like wills and insurance? We all know we are going to die at some point, right? We just don't want to be reminded of that fact until later down the line. However, what happens to your loved ones in the event you suffer an untimely death? Will your family have enough money to pay for your funeral plus the other bills in your absence? Will your family be able to get the assets you leave behind, or would you rather the courts make that decision? This is why it's important to put a plan in motion now.

WHAT IS ESTATE PLANNING?

In its simplest yet comprehensive definition, estate planning is a process by which you spell out your wishes in case something unfortunate happens to you, like death. Most people start the process by writing a will. This is a legal document that lists your instructions after your death, such as who gets your assets if you die; who will pay your bills; or who will care for your children if they are not adults at the time of your passing. Estate planning may also help with other issues, such as minimizing estate taxes or providing for a child with special needs.

The Importance of a Will

In life we accumulate many material "things," some of which may have monetary value, while others don't. It makes sense to have a legal plan in place to make sure that the people you want to receive your assets actually get them when you are no longer here. Clearly spelling out those thoughts in a will can help your loved ones go through this time with as little difficulty as possible. If you don't have a will, the courts will make decisions as to the distribution of your assets based on the laws of your state. Some people put off getting a will because they feel they don't have anything of real value. However, if you own a car or a house, plus retirement savings, you are probably worth more than you think.

Hire an estate planning attorney to draw up your will. There are software packages you can buy and Web sites that promise to create a do-it-yourself will, but they may not contain all the necessary parts that are required by your state to be considered legal. Wills are not very expensive, but prices vary by attorney. You may get one for as cheap as $100 for a simple one or pay more for a more complex case. After you have your will, make sure to put it in a secure place such as a safety deposit or lock box, but more importantly, remember where you put it. Also make sure your executor, the personal representative you name in the will, will carry out your instructions and knows where the will is in case something happens to you.

You should review your will every three or four years to make sure it's up to date. For example, you might have created the will before you got married and started a family, but now need to add a spouse and children. Maybe you had a favorite nephew you planned to leave something to, but now wish to cut him out because he is always bugging you for money. It may turn out that you need to replace your will altogether. Along the same lines, make sure you update your beneficiary designations on insurance policies and retirement plans to make sure the person you name receives the proceeds. For instance, if you go through a messy divorce, your ex-spouse could be in for a huge windfall if you fail to update those records.

Living Will/Healthcare Power of Attorney

We never want to think about the fact we may be too ill to make our own health decisions, but there have been several high-profile cases over the years in which this happened. Let's say you were in a car accident that leaves you unconscious and one of your arms crushed. The doctor can save the arm from amputation, but a decision needs to be made right away on the course of action.

A healthcare power of attorney is a document that allows you to give someone else the power to make decisions regarding your health in the event you are deemed unable to do so. The person you designate should be someone who knows your values and whom you trust because there is a chance they could decide whether you live or die. It can be extremely difficult to tell the doctors to stop providing food or care for a loved one, so you may want to name an alternate person as well in case the person you choose is unwilling to make a decision or is unavailable.

When you name your healthcare power of attorney, go ahead and get a living will, too. This is a document that expresses your wishes in the event you are terminally ill. It lets your doctors know if you wish to continue having feeding tubes or other means of prolonging your life even if there is no chance of you ever recovering.

Some states use a document called an Advanced Health Care Directive, which is a combination of a living will and healthcare power of attorney. This way, you don't have to worry about keeping track of two separate documents. You also don't necessarily have to have a lawyer prepare these documents for you because each state has its own forms where you can fill in the blanks. Many of us put things off to a later date and forget. These are important documents that you need to have now!

One more document to add to your arsenal is a power of attorney form. A healthcare power of attorney only covers health matters, but in the event you become incapacitated, who will pay your bills or handle other financial matters? A durable or springing power of attorney can help. A springing power of attorney takes effect only when you become incapacitated. Not all states recognize springing power of attorney documents, so check with your state before getting one.

A durable power of attorney becomes effective the day it is signed. It's important to choose this person carefully because he or she can control your assets. The agent you name will have the ability to handle things such as:

- Conduct real estate transactions
- Banking transactions
- Making investment decisions
- Giving gifts on your behalf

A durable or springing power of attorney will not give you authority to make healthcare choices if you are deemed incapable of doing so. Therefore, it's important to make sure you have the appropriate documents in place to delegate those decisions. Many estate planning attorneys offer package deals to create a will, living will, healthcare power of attorney and durable power of attorney to make it affordable. However, even if it costs a few hundred dollars, wouldn't it be nice to know that the instructions are already in place so that your wishes are carried out if you are unable to make decisions on your own?

LIFE INSURANCE

If you have no dependents, then you probably don't need life insurance because it is typically meant to take care of the family you leave behind. Life insurance, sometimes referred to as life assurance, provides for a payment of a sum of money upon the death of the insured. In addition, life insurance can be used as a means of investment or saving.

There are basically two types of life insurance: term and permanent. Let's start off with term life insurance.

Term Insurance

Term insurance is temporary insurance. It will pay a benefit if the insured person dies during a specified period of time. So if you purchased a twenty-year term policy in 2007 and you die in 2015, the insurance company would pay the claim, assuming your premium payments were current and you did nothing to violate any terms of the policy. However, if you pass away in 2029 and fail to renew your policy, the insurance company would not pay. Term insurance is good if you purchase a policy while you are young because the premiums are generally less than an whole life insurance policy. One disadvantage, however, is that the premiums you pay do not go toward building wealth like a permanent policy. Some term policies do refund the premiums at the end of the period, but they cost a little more. Also, if you do not die during the term and decide to renew the policy, it will be more expensive because you are now older and the insurance company is essentially issuing a new one based on your current age.

You may have heard some financial advisors use the phrase, *"Buy term and invest the rest."* If you are in your twenties or thirties, this strategy may make sense. Jordan is a thirty-year-old female in pretty decent health. She can get a thirty-year term insurance policy worth $300,000 for about $30 per month. By comparison, a whole life policy would cost about $210 monthly. If Jordan invests the additional $180 per month in an S&P 500 Index Fund, she can expect to earn a return that matches the stock market. Historically, this index has risen 10% annually. If that rate continues, Jordan would have more than $400,000 in that account. At the end of her term, she would have more than the insurance policy was worth to begin with. At that point she may decide that she doesn't need to renew the coverage, and she can then use that investment account as her insurance policy. Or, she could decide to get a smaller amount of coverage because she has already built up a sizable nest egg. If you decide to go this route, make sure you have the discipline to put that extra money aside religiously every month. It may also be a good idea to set up monthly payments through online banking so you don't have to think about mailing a check.

Permanent Insurance

When you buy permanent insurance, you are buying a product that consists of a death benefit and a savings account. The death benefit works similarly to a term policy that pays your loved ones in the event you die. However, the savings account allows you to create wealth. A portion of your monthly premium goes toward the death benefit and the remaining is deposited in an account that is invested in conservative investments like government bonds. Universal life is similar to whole life except that it allows you to use the interest you have earned from the savings account to apply towards premiums. This can help ensure your coverage doesn't lapse in case you face an unexpected cash crunch. In addition, there is also variable life insurance which provides more flexibility of investment options. You can invest in stocks, bonds or mutual funds with this type of policy. The benefit is that if your investments go up, it increases the value of your policy. The downside is that if your investments go down, it can decrease the death benefit paid to your heirs.

You could use the strategy above outlined for term insurance and save on costs. It's not uncommon for an insurance agent to receive a commission equal to your first year's premium for a whole life policy, which makes it very expensive.

There is an old saying that it's called "whole life insurance" because you pay premiums on permanent life policies for your entire life. However, that is changing now. Many insurance companies offer products where you can pay for the policy in a lump sum payment or pay it off over a set period of time, such as ten or twenty years. This type of product is helpful to the person who wants to provide his family with a benefit that is certain unlike a term policy, which won't pay if you outlive that period.

How Much Insurance Do You Need?

Figuring out how much insurance you will need is no simple task. If you are the breadwinner of your family, you will certainly want to provide your loved ones with enough to pay for their essential needs if you aren't around. Your insurance needs will also change as time passes. Today you may not have a family, but five years from now that could change. As your children grow up and your assets increase, the need to provide for your heirs may decrease.

There are a couple of ways to determine how much insurance to purchase: using the human needs approach and the capital preservation approach.

With the human needs approach, you need to determine how much your family will need to sustain their lifestyle after you are gone. Include estimates of the costs of funeral expenses, probate fees, medical costs, housing, child care, education costs, debts and any essential monthly bills. To figure out this number, add up all of your household expenses such as food, bills, insurance costs (car, health, etc.), and any other essential monthly costs. Multiply this number by 12 to get an estimate of your annual costs.

Next, determine how many years you would like the insurance proceeds to cover and multiply your yearly costs by this number. Finally, add any final expenses such as probate fees and funeral costs as well as an estimate for college costs for your children, and this will give you an estimate of how much coverage you'll need using the human needs approach.

The chart below illustrates how to calculate such an estimate. Molly is 50 years old and is looking for expense coverage for fifteen years, at which time she plans to retire and can begin collecting social security. The actual figure was $668,100. Sounds like a lot of money, right? Next, you subtract any retirement assets. She and her husband have a total of $160,000 in IRAs and 401(k) accounts, bringing the balance down roughly $500,000.

The capital preservation approach works similarly. However, the goal is to "preserve" the death benefit from the insurance and live off the interest. So, using the example above, if Molly receives $500,000, she will invest the funds and only withdraw any earnings. If her investments earn $50,000, bringing her balance to $550,000, she could withdraw $50,000, thus "preserving" her $500,000 of "capital." However, she could choose to only take out $40,000. Earnings will fluctuate from year to year as the chart below illustrates, so it is important to make you follow a budget to control overspending. Using this approach ensures that Molly will have assets to pass to her children or donate to charity upon her death.

Burial Insurance

Funerals can be expensive. When my dad passed away in 2006, his funeral service cost almost $9,000, including burial fees. According to a National Funeral Directors Association

Human Needs Example

Bill	Monthly	Yearly
Mortgage	$ 1,200	$ 14,400
Food	$ 300	$ 3,600
Car insurance	$ 140	$ 1,680
Health insurance	$ 400	$ 4,800
Utilities	$ 200	$ 2,400
Childcare	$ 350	$ 4,200
Church/Charity	$ 300	$ 3,600
Car payment	$ 300	$ 3,600
Phone/Cell	$ 100	$ 1,200
Cable	$ 80	$ 960
Total	$ 3,370	$ 40,440

Funeral	$ 8,500
Probate	$ 3,000
College	$ 50,000
Additional Costs	$ 61,500

15 year of expenses	$ 606,600
Additional Costs	$ 61,500
Total	$ 668,100
Minus retirement assets	$ 160,000
Human needs estimate	$ 508,100

survey, the average cost of a funeral in 2006 was approximately $7,300, not including burial expense. If your children are grown or you have no dependents, you probably don't need a lot of insurance. You may just want to have enough to cover your burial expenses if you don't have enough savings to cover the costs. You could purchase a life insurance policy in the amount that you think your funeral will cost.

Another option is to purchase a pre-arranged funeral package. This can remove a huge financial burden for your family and make sure you get the funeral you desire. The funds used for pre-paid funerals are usually held at a financial institution. Make sure it is a reputable one that is FDIC-insured. It's also very important to understand what you are paying for: If you want to a casket and flowers, make sure that is included in the contract and delete those items you do not want. Also check to see if the plan can be transferred if you move to another city.

Other Considerations

If you plan to get life insurance, it's always better to get it earlier in life than later. This kind of thing is not something that most people are eager to approach, but it's a practical life situation, and because we never know when we will die, quite literally, handle this today – don't wait.

Also, each day you wait causes your policy to go up in price because as you age, funeral prices go up. In addition, if you have health problems later in life it will make it even more expensive.

Consider adding an inflation rider to your policy. This will make sure that the $500,000 policy you purchased today will be worth a similar or same amount in the future when your beneficiaries make a claim.

Capital Presentation Example

	Beginning Balance	Interest Earned	Ending Balance	Withdrawal
Year 1	$ 500,000	$ 50,000	$ 550,000	$ 50,000
Year 2	$ 500,000	$ 35,000	$ 535,000	$ 30,000
Year 3	$ 505,000	$ 40,000	$ 545,000	$ 30,000
Year 4	$ 515,000	$ 25,000	$ 540,000	$ 32,000
Year 5	$ 508,000	$ 30,000	$ 538,000	$ 30,000
Year 6	$ 508,000	$ 33,000	$ 541,000	$ 35,000
Year 7	$ 506,000	$ 15,000	$ 521,000	$ 21,000
Year 8	$ 500,000	$ 39,000	$ 539,000	$ 15,000
Year 9	$ 524,000	$ 25,000	$ 549,000	$ 49,000
Year 10	$ 500,000			

Things to Remember

1. Get an estate plan today if you don't have one.

2. Review your plan every three or four years to make sure it is up to date

3. Update your beneficiaries to make sure you are leaving insurance or retirement assets to the people you wish.

4. Don't put off getting insurance because premiums go up as you get older.

CHAPTER 14

THE GOLDEN YEARS

Following the plans laid out in the previous chapters can help you achieve the kind of retirement you seek.

Hey, it's a red-letter day! Retirement has finally arrived! No more work. The kids are hopefully out of the house. Now is the time to enjoy life a little. Maybe your plan is to travel more or visit and spoil your grandchildren or just sit around all day and do nothing.

RETIREMENT SPENDING

If you are 59 ½ or older, you can now make withdrawals from Traditional and Roth IRAs without a penalty. If you set up your Roth IRA at least five years ago, you have an extra benefit once you reach retirement age: no taxes on withdrawals. Since you invested after tax dollars in the account as you were building it up, the government views you as having paid your taxes.

Now, if you have a traditional IRA, rollover IRA, or funds in some kind of qualified retirement plan like a 401(k) or 403(b), you will have to pay taxes on your distributions. This is because you most likely received a tax break for contributions into these accounts (unless you made non-deductible contributions), so now the government can grab its share it has waited all these years to get. If you no longer work and totally live off your retirement funds, then you probably are in a lower tax bracket than when you were in the workforce, and the IRS will tax you based on the rate at the time you begin taking your money.

For example, if you are 60 years old and the income from your job places you in the 28% tax bracket, you would pay $2,800 on a $10,000 withdrawal from your traditional IRA. You would pay $1,500 on that distribution if you are retired and this is the only source of income because it places you in the in 15% tax bracket. Also, with Traditional IRAs, if you haven't begun withdrawing funds by age 70 ½, you will be subject to extra taxes! Yes, it's true! They'll even tax you if you don't withdraw your own funds – at this age!

If you have a Roth IRA and a Traditional IRA, it's a good idea to withdraw from the Roth first since there are no taxes after retirement age.

DETERMINING HOW MUCH TO WITHDRAW

You need to determine how much your living expenses are and build in some wiggle room because health care coverage gets more expensive as you get older. Now is a good time to go back to the table at the end of Chapter 1 and revise your budget.

One rule of thumb regarding withdrawing funds from retirement accounts is to take 4% each year. The rationale is that this should allow your funds to last at least twenty-five years. According to a 2006 report issued from the Centers for Disease Control and Prevention, someone 60 years old can expect to live an additional twenty-three years. So if the government's math is correct, you will spend about 25% of your life in retirement. If you have paid enough in Social Security taxes, you can start to withdraw at age 62, which can help defray some costs. If a 4% withdrawal won't cover your expenses, you can consider increasing to 5%, but you don't want to increase the percentage so that you will deplete your savings over a short period of time.

In recent years some experts have suggested that withdrawing 6% annually can help maintain your lifestyle, but there are risks. Pundits talk about owning anywhere from 65% to 80% of your retirement portfolio in stocks. This goes against the age-based approach outlined in Chapter 12 because as you get older, the stock portion of the portfolio will decline. This is to prevent heavy losses due to wild stock market swings. It's probably not prudent for an 80-year-old to have an investment portfolio with 80% in stocks.

The chart below shows the impact of having 80% of a $200,000 portfolio in the Vanguard Total Bond Fund and 20% in the Vanguard 500 Index (a stock fund that invests in the S&P 500 stocks) from 1998 to 2008. As you can see, the stock fund was down 13.74% over that time period. In the first table, using the 80% stock/20% bond allocation would have increased the portfolio by only $5,464 over the ten-year time period, which isn't very much income. Using the age-based method, the portfolio would have grown by more than $100,000.

Also, during the time period of this example, the stock market experienced one of its sharpest downturns, so this isn't indicative of historical returns, but the point is that when more of your funds are tied to stock market performance in retirement years, you potentially put your lifestyle at risk. A younger person still working has time on his side to make up for stock market losses, but the retired person living off their savings and Social Security doesn't have that luxury.

80% STOCKS/20% BONDS

Mutual Fund	Return	Allocation	Beginning	Gain/Loss	Ending
Vanguard S&P 500	-13.75%	80%	$ 160,000	$ (22,000)	$ 138,000
Vanguard Total Bond	68.66%	20%	$ 40,000	$ 27,464	$ 67,464
Total			$ 200,000		$ 205,464

20% STOCKS/ 80% BONDS

Mutual Fund	Return	Allocation	Beginning	Gain/Loss	Ending
Vanguard S&P 500	-13.75%	20%	$ 40,000	$ (5,500)	$ 34,500
Vanguard Total Bond	68.66%	80%	$ 160,000	$ 109,856	$ 269,856
Total			$ 200,000		$ 304,356

SOCIAL SECURITY

The federal government initiated the Social Security program in 1935. The purpose of the program is to have employees and their employers pay taxes during their working years which will then be used to pay a monthly benefit once retirement age is reached or if a serious disability occurs.

Companies and their employees each contribute 7.65% of the worker's wages, which also includes 1.45% for Medicare hospital insurance (which will be discussed later). To be eligible to receive retirement benefits, you need to have earned forty credits, which works out to ten years of work (because you can earn a maximum of four credits per year). You can receive reduced retirement benefits at age 62 and maximum benefits at age 70. For disability benefits, you generally need to have earned at least twenty credits (five years of work) before becoming eligible.

There are also special provisions in the Social Security system to provide survivor benefits for widows and children of the deceased up to a certain age.

Social Security can help defray costs during retirement. According to the U.S. Social Security Administration, the average monthly social security benefit in 2009 was $1,153, or about $12,000 annually. Generally, if social security is the only source of your income, it's not taxable and you don't have to file a tax return. In 2008, if you were single and collecting Social Security, the benefit is tax-exempt if your total income was less than $25,000 (or $32,000 for couples).

There is no right or wrong answer to the question, "When is the best time to start collecting my Social Security?" Some choose to start at 62 and continue to let their IRAs and other retirement accounts accumulate, while others chose to wait until they get older so they can draw a larger amount from the government. The Social Security Administration has a wealth of resources on its Web site (http://www.ssa.gov/retire2) to help answer questions on benefits and how to apply, or you can call 800-772-1213 for more information.

MEDICARE

In addition to the government's retirement benefits, it also provides health insurance coverage through Medicare. Created in 1965, this program provides health insurance for those 65 and older as well as some people younger than 65 with certain disabilities. Medicare has four parts: *Part A, Part B, Part C (Medicare Advantage), and Part D.*

ENROLLMENT PERIOD

It's important to understand the enrollment periods for Medicare, because it can cost you higher premiums if you fail to sign up when first eligible. The enrollment period is a seven-month window of time. It begins three months before your 65th birthday, includes the month of your birthday and the three months after your birthday. If you elect to receive Social Security before your 65th birthday, you will be automatically enrolled in Part A, but you will still have to elect whether to receive Part B. If you choose not to sign up for Part B, you have to wait until open enrollment the next year, from January 1 through March 31.

If you choose to enroll in Part B after the initial eligibility period, you may be subject to higher premiums, which are 10% higher for each year that you delay enrollment. For example, if you turned 65 in 2008 and decided to sign up for Part B in 2009, you would have to pay a monthly premium of $106.04 per month ($96.40 monthly premium plus a $9.64 penalty) compared to $96.40 for those who enrolled when eligible. This penalty will continue to be paid as long as you are enrolled in Part B, but remember: this coverage is optional.

The penalty was put in place to prevent adverse selection, which is meant to discourage people from signing up when a health problem occurs after the initial open enrollment period. There are special circumstances in which the penalty doesn't apply, such as if you continue to work beyond age 65 and are covered through a group plan on your job.

Part A

Medicare Part A is known as hospital insurance. It will help cover inpatient care in a hospital, skilled nursing care facility, hospice, and home care in some situations. The hospital stays cover costs associated with your visit such as room, meals, and hospital services and supplies. This insurance does not provide coverage for long-term or custodial care, which will be discussed later. Skilled nursing care is included and is defined as care to maintain or improve your current health status. This type of care is usually provided in a nursing home.

A benefit period begins the first day you go into a hospital or skilled nursing facility. This benefit period can last up to 100 days for Home Health Coverage. The first twenty days are free, but each additional day up to 100 is $133.50 per day. The deductible for hospital stays in 2009 is $1,068. This cost will cover the first sixty days of inpatient care at a Medicare-approved hospital. After you have been out of the Medicare approved facility for 60 days or longer you can get a new benefit period, but you will have to pay another deductible. If by chance you need a hospital stay lasting more than 90 days you will tap into a 60 day lifetime reserve. Each person only receives one lifetime reserve. Once it has been exhausted you can't receive another one. Below is a table showing the coinsurance, out of pocket costs, for hospital and skilled nursing facility stays for Medicare Part A in 2009.

Part A Coinsurance	Cost per day
1 – 60	$0
61 – 90	$267
91 – 150	$534

Skilled Nursing	Cost per day
1 – 20	0
21 – 100	$133.50

Hospice Care is provided for terminally ill patients. Medicare defines terminally ill as those expecting to live six months or less. You can receive care for longer than six months if approved by a Medicare provider. Respite care is also covered. This means the government will pay for someone to see about a patient so the usual caregiver can have a break. Most people do not pay premiums for Medicare Part A because they paid Medicare taxes while they were working.

Part B

Medicare Part B is known as medical insurance and covers medical services such as doctor's fees and outpatient care that Part A does not pay. Part B is optional. It is primarily used for doctor visits, but also covers outpatient physical and occupational therapy, chiropractic care, outpatient mental health services, X-rays and labs, and durable medical equipment like canes and scooters. It does not cover eyeglasses, hearing aids, dental care, or long-term care. The monthly premium for 2009 is $96.40 for married couples with an annual income under $170,000, and for single individuals making less than $85,000. If you make more than those levels, you will pay more. In addition to the monthly premium, you will pay an annual deductible, which is $135 in 2009. After meeting the deductible, you will generally pay 20% of the costs.

Assignment

Before jumping on to Part C, it's important to talk about assignment. If a physician agrees to assignment, it means they accept payments directly from Medicare and will agree to accept the Medicare-approved amount, the cost of which Medicare pays, as payment in full and can not add additional charges. Health care providers do have the option of not accepting assignment, which gives them the right to charge an additional 15% above the Medicare-approved amount. You also may be asked to pay the entire bill up front and wait for Medicare to reimburse you.

The table below illustrates an example of the cost of two doctors, one accepting assignment and one not. As you can see, the orthopedic doctor charges $125 for an office visit. Medicare will pay $100, which leaves you with a $20 charge (20% of $100) if he accepts assignment. The doctor who doesn't accept assignment can charge an additional $15 (15% of 100) on top of the $20 co-insurance, bringing the bill to $35. So be sure to ask doctors if they accept assignment before making appointments.

Orthopedic Doctor	Doctor Charge	Medicare-Approved Amount	Your Cost
Accepts Assignment	$125	$100	$20
Declines Assignment	$125	$100	$35

Medicare Advantage (Part C)

In addition to Medicare Parts A and B, some choose to join Medicare Advantage Plans (Part C). These are voluntary health insurance plans offered by private insurance companies to provide additional coverage not provided under Part A and Part B. These are Health Maintenance Organizations (HMOs), Preferred Provider Organizations (PPOs), Private Fee-for-Service Plans, and Special Needs Plans, which require a monthly premium, but the co-payments for services are typically less than those under the Original Medicare Plans (Part A and B). These plans also typically offer prescription coverage (Plan D).

Patients using this insurance will be in a network and must use doctors and hospitals that are included in that plan. You must be signed up for Part A and B to be eligible to get a Medicare Advantage policy. If you decide to go this route, think carefully about your needs ahead of time to best decide which company can provide the coverage you desire and that also fits your budget.

Types of Medicare Advantage Plans

Health Maintenance Organization (HMO) – With this form of health insurance, you are limited to seeing only those providers in the network. Primary care doctors serve as gatekeepers and must approve all visits to specialists. In most cases there is no coverage for appointments with doctors outside the network. The coordination of care is designed to improve communication among your medical professionals and help drive down costs. Doctors in an HMO are typically paid a monthly fee regardless of whether you have a visit.

Preferred Provider Organization (PPO) – This is similar to an HMO, but care is not paid in advance. Doctors and hospitals in the network, which is usually larger than an HMO network, agree to provide services at a reduced rate to patients in the network. You don't need a referral to see a specialist in a PPO, but the co-payment may be higher than for a visit to your primary care physician.

Private Fee-for-Service Plans (PFFS) – These plans give the most freedom as far as choosing a medical provider, but they also have higher co-payments and deductibles compared with HMOs and PPOs. Usually, patients will pay doctors directly for services and submit a claim to the insurance company for reimbursement.

Special Needs Plans – This category of plans was created to cater to patients with chronic diseases such as diabetes or HIV/AIDS. One way of thinking about these plans is that they are "specialized HMOs." You will be limited to a certain network of providers, but they will be focused only on specific illnesses. You do have to obtain a referral in most cases to see a specialist with this type of plan.

Part D

As you can tell from this section of the book, Medicare isn't the easiest system to learn. It does take time and patience to go through these plans, but I advise you strongly to do so with a fine-toothed comb, because this is your health we're talking about.

Now we'll move on to the next letter in the alphabet, Part D. This is prescription drug coverage, which helps subsidize costs. If you are in a Medicare Advantage plan, you do not need to purchase a stand-alone prescription because you are already covered, but also remember that Part D is optional. There are many different plans from which to choose. Some are limited to certain groups of drugs, which can be more cost-effective, while others are more comprehensive and more expensive. You will also want to think about the cost. The deductible in 2009 can't exceed $295. Some plans have no deductibles. If you have expensive prescriptions, you probably want to consider plans that offer additional coverage because most plans have a coverage gap, a range at which you pay 100% of the costs. In 2009, that gap is between $2,700 and $4,350. Medicare's Web site (http://www.medicare.gov) has some valuable tools that will allow you to compare different stand-alone prescription plans as well as Medicare Advantage. Be sure to check it out to help with your evaluation process.

Medicare Supplements (Medigap)

Because Medicare doesn't cover all of your healthcare needs, private companies offer supplemental policies to fill in the "gaps." There are twelve different standardized supplemental plans offered in this category.

So, we're going to add more letters of the alphabet, for these twelve standardized plans: A – L. All plans have to offer the same core benefits, so for example Plan A covers Part A co-payments for hospital stays from day 61 to day 90. Every insurance company selling a Plan A policy must have this benefit. Also, these plans cannot duplicate benefits in Medicare Part A and Part B. Prices will vary according to the plan you choose. Plan J (which will be phased out in 2010), which currently has the most comprehensive coverage, will cost more than Plan A, which has minimal benefits.

Long-Term Care Insurance

There are many healthcare options for seniors within the Medicare system; however, it may not cover all of your needs, even with the supplemental plans. If you need custodial care, such as assistance with daily living activities such as bathing and eating, you should consider purchasing long-term care insurance. Medicare only covers skilled nursing care, which is typically provided in an approved facility. You may not need that level of assistance and wish to remain in your own home. Also, Medicare doesn't provide coverage, in most cases, for nursing home care. Long-term care policies can help alleviate some of those costs. This type of insurance can be affordable if all you need is someone to help out a few hours a day with things like getting dressed, preparing meals, and bathing, but it can be very expensive if you need nursing home care.

As with everything, it's important to do some research to prevent buying a product you will not use. For example, if you want to stay at home, you may not need a policy with nursing home benefits. It is also probably a good idea to add inflation protection to your coverage, which will provide a worthwhile benefit when you start making claims. And, as with any other insurance, it's best to purchase this when you are younger to get lower premiums and before you have a health problem, because you could be denied otherwise.

Things to Remember

1. You can make penalty-free withdrawals from IRAs at age 59 ½.

2. Try to limit annual withdrawals from retirement accounts to 4% to 5% of the total value of your account.

3. Social Security provides a retirement benefit to those 62 and older who have paid into the system as well as younger people who have a disability.

4. The Medicare system is a comprehensive one that provides hospital, medical and prescription coverage.

5. Supplemental plans and long-term care insurance can fill in some of the costs that Medicare doesn't cover.

Resources

BANKING

Federal Deposit Insurance Corporation
1776 F St, N.W.
Washington, DC. 20006
877-275-3342
Supervises banks and insures deposits in these institutions up to $250,000
http://www.fdic.gov/index.html

National Credit Union Administration
1775 Duke St.
Alexandria, VA. 22314-3428
703-518-6300
Supervises credit unions and insures deposits up to $250,000
http://www.ncua.gov

CREDIT

Federal Reserve Board
20th Street and Constitution Avenue, N.W.
Washington, DC. 20551
This link provides useful tips on shopping for a credit card
http://www.federalreserve.gov/pubs/shop

Equifax
PO Box 740241
Atlanta, GA. 30374
800-685-1111
http://www.equifax.com

Experian
PO Box 2104
Allen, TX 75013-2104
888-397-3742
http://www.experian.com

Trans Union
PO Box 2000
Chester, PA. 19022
800-888-4213
http://www.transunion.com/index.jsp

FICO Score estimate
http://www.bankrate.com/brm/fico/calc.asp

National Score Index
Provides national and regional averages of credit scores.
http://www.nationalscoreindex.com/

AnnualCreditReport.com
PO Box 105283
Atlanta, GA. 30348-5283
877-322-8228
Centralized source for obtaining credit reports from the 3 major credit bureaus.
http://www.annualcreditreport.com

National Foundation for Credit Counseling
801 Roeder Rd.
Suite 900
Silver Spring, MD. 20910
800-388-2227
Information on credit counseling
http://www.nfcc.org

Credit Repair Organizations Act of 1996
Details laws governing Credit Repair firms
http://www.ftc.gov/os/statutes/croa/croa.htm

Fair Credit Reporting Act
Information on the laws protecting consumers
http://www.ftc.gov/os/statutes/fcrajump.shtm

Center for Responsible Lending
302 West Main St.
Durham, NC 27701
919-313-8500
Organization working to put an end to predatory lending practices
http://www.responsiblelending.org

IDENTITY THEFT

Verified by Visa
Provides information on its program to protect consumers
buying products on the Internet
https://usa.visa.com/personal/security/vbv

National Do Not Call Registry
Attn: DNC Program Manager
Federal Trade Commission
600 Pennsylvania Ave, N.W.
Washington, DC. 20580
Add your home and cell phone to this list to limit telemarketer calls
888-382-1222
https://www.donotcall.gov/default.aspx

Privacy Rights Clearinghouse
3100 - 5th Ave., Suite B
San Diego, CA 92103
Phone: (619) 298-3396
http://www.privacyrights.org

Identity Theft Resource Center
PO Box 26833
San Diego, CA. 92196
858-693-7935
Nonprofit organization focusing exclusively on identity theft
http://www.idtheftcenter.org/alerts.shtml

PHISHING EMAILS

Anti-Phishing Working Group
http://www.antiphishing.org/index.html

Hoax-Slayer
http://www.hoax-slayer.com

JOB INFORMATION

Personality tests

Keirsey Temperament Sorter II
http://www.keirsey.com

Jung-Myers Briggs
http://www.humanmetrics.com

Job Web Sites

Monster.com
5 Clock Tower Pl
#500
Maynard, MA 01754
800-666-7837
http://www.monster.com

Careerbuilder.com
200 N. Lasalle St
Suite 1100
Chicago, IL. 60601
866-438-1485
http://careerbuilder.com

Yahoo Hotjobs
45 W. 18th St
6th Floor
New York, NY. 10011
646-351-5300
http://hotjobs.yahoo.com

Internship Opportunities

MonsterTrak
5 Clock Tower Pl, Suite 500
Maynard, MA 01754
http://www.monstertrak.com

INROADS, Inc
10 South Broadway, Suite 300
St. Louis, MO. 63102
314-241-7488
http://www.inroads.org

InternWeb
http://www.internweb.com

Entreprenuer
SCORE
409 3rd St, S.W.
6th Floor
Washington, DC 20024
800-634-0245
http://www.score.org

Entrepreneurs' Organization
500 Montgomery St
Suite 500
Alexandria, VA 22314 USA
703-519-6700
http://www.eonetwork.org

EDUCATION

The College Board
Source for information on preparing for college
45 Columbus Ave
New York, NY 10023-6992
(212) 713-8000
http://www.collegeboard.com

Diploma Mills
Information on how to spot diploma mills
http://www.elearners.com/resources/diploma-mills.asp

Council for Higher Education Accreditation
One Dupont Cir, N.W.
Suite 510
Washington, DC. 20036
202-955-6126
List of accredited online programs by state
http://www.chea.org/degreemills/frmStates.htm

National Endowment for Financial Education
5299 DTC Blvd
Suite 1300
Greenwood Village, CO. 80111
303-741-6333
Non-profit that has programs designed to teach consumers about personal finance
http://www.nefe.org

JumpStart Coalition for Personal Financial Literacy
919 18th St, N.W.
Suite 300
Washington, DC. 20006
202-466-8604
Seeks to improve financial literacy of young adults
http://www.jumpstart.org

Junior Achievement
One Education Way
Colorado Springs, CO. 80906
800-843-6395
Educates students in grades K-12 about opportunities available in the business world
http://www.ja.org

HOUSING/CAR BUYING

U.S. Department of Housing and Urban Development
451 7th St., S.W.
Washington, DC. 20410
(202) 708-1112
Useful home buying tips
http://www.hud.gov/buying/index.cfm#programs

Fannie Mae
3900 Wisconsin Ave, N.W.
Washington, DC. 20016-2892
800-732-6643
Offers financial products to make housing affordable for low to middle income families
www.fanniemae.com

Carfax.com
Provides vehicle history reports that cover collision, fire, and flood damage
http://www.carfax.com

Edmunds.com
Comprehensive source for on buying new or used vehicles as well as leasing.
http://www.edmunds.com

Kelley Blue Book
195 Technology
Irvine, CA. 92618
800-258-3266
Find the estimated wholesale and retail value of your vehicle
http://www.kbb.com

LemonLawOffice.com
Provides lemon law information for each of the 50 states and a list of lawyers who represent clients who are victims
http://www.lemonlawoffice.com

HomeGain
1250 45th St.
Suite 200
Emeryville, CA. 94608
888-542-0800
Website helps buyers and sellers find real estate agents
http://www.homegain.com

INVESTING

Sharebuilder
1445 – 120th Ave, N.E.
Bellevue, WA. 98005
8600747-2537
Allows investors to buy stocks with no minimum account size.
http://www.sharebuilder.com

NYSE Euronext
11 Wall St.
New York, NY. 10005
212-656-3000
Information on Exchange Traded Funds
http://www.amex.com/etf/EtMain.jsp

MUTUAL FUND INFORMATION

Morningstar
22 W. Washington St
Chicago, IL. 60602
312-696-6000
http://www.morningstar.com

Lipper
3 Times Sq
New York, NY. 10036
877-955-4773
http://www.lipperweb.com

RETIREMENT CALCULATORS

Bankrate.com
11760 US HWY 1
Suite 500
North Palm Beach, FL. 33408
561-630-2400
http://www.bankrate.com/brm/calc/401k.asp

Banksite.com
http://www.banksite.com/calc/annuity2

PERSONAL FINANCE WEB SITES

Yahoo Finance
http://finance.yahoo.com

MSN Money Central
http://moneycentral.msn.com

TAXES

Internal Revenue Service
1111 Constitution Ave., N.W.
Washington, DC. 20224
800-829-1040
Provides comprehensive source for tax information
http://www.irs.gov/individuals/index.html

Medicare
Centers for Medicare & Medicaid Services
7500 Security Blvd
Baltimore, MD. 21244-1850
800-633-4227
http://www.medicare.gov

SOCIAL SECURITY

Social Security Administration
Office of Public Inquiries
Windsor Park Building
6401 Security Blvd.
Baltimore, MD 21235
800-772-1213
http://www.ssa.gov

EPILOGUE

Managing your finances today is more complicated than ever before. It is about more than getting lucky and scoring big on a piece of real estate or finding that hot stock that goes up 500% in one year. Those things can happen, but more times than not success comes from pulling up your sleeves and doing hard work.

You can have that comfortable retirement you are seeking, but it will require making some choices regarding your lifestyle today. You will need to save and invest diligently in the upturns and downturns the markets go through. If you are in a financial hole right now, don't be discouraged. You can get yourself out. You are now armed with some tools that can help guide you whether you are young or old or whether you are on solid financial ground or not.

Thank you for reading my book. I would love to hear from you. Tell me what you enjoyed and what I can improve upon. Email me at info@mapyourfinancialfuture.com or write letters to the address below.

Lyons Den Press
PO Box 1341
Durham, North Carolina 27702

About the Author

Patrick Lyons

has more than 15 years of experience as an investment professional. Lyons earned a B.S. in Mathematics from Florida A&M University and an M.S. in Management (Finance Concentration) from North Carolina State University. He is the author of *Map Your Financial Future: Starting the Right Path in Your Teens and Twenties.* His investment and personal finance advice has been featured in the Wall Street Transcript, The News & Observer (Raleigh, NC), Black Enterprise magazine and various radio and television shows. Lyons has also taught business finance at Wake Technical Community College and conducted workshops on personal finance for several schools and organizations.

INDEX

B

D

E

H

I

J

K

L

M

N

O

P

R

T

U

V

W

www.ingramcontent.com/pod-product-compliance
Lightning Source LLC
Chambersburg PA
CBHW020201200326
41521CB00005BA/211